Things people ar...

SHAME UNMASKED

"*Shame Unmasked* is a brave, challenging, and necessary work to anyone who really wants to live a life of freedom. This book is a helpful companion for the journey."

— **Fr. Richard Rohr, O.F.M.,**
Founder of the Center for Action and Contemplation

"Shame can terrorize you and strip you of all that you are and can be. Thankfully, Rick Patterson exposes shame for what it is and helps all of us to reclaim our lives. **A must read.**"

— **S. Renee Smith,**
Nationally recognized self-esteem & branding expert,
coach, speaker, and coauthor of *Self-Esteem for Dummies*

"Shame takes on all forms of negative self-talk. Richard Patterson explores all aspects of shame in his groundbreaking new book. Through his own stories and those of his brave children, **Richard takes the reader on an eye-opening adventure of self-discovery.**"

— **Danette Kubanda,**
Emmy Award-winning television producer, publicity consultant,
media coach, and writer, Danette Kubanda Media & PR

"Rick Patterson shows how shame distorts all our relationships, and he points us to the path of healing and wholeness—**an important book for all those who deep down feel that they are not good enough.**"

— **Dr. Tom Boogaart,**
Professor of Old Testament,
Western Theological Seminary

SHAME
UNMASKED

Disarming The Hidden Driver
Behind Our Destructive Decisions

RICK PATTERSON

Printed in the United States of America
First Printing: April 2017

978-0-9988753-0-9 (paper)
978-0-9988753-1-6 (ebook)
CFC Publishing

*This book is dedicated to those
in whom I see myself...*

LOOKING FORWARD:

Troy, Tilonda, TiShanté, and Tapricia McGuffey

LOOKING BACK:

Russell C. Weaver

Contents

PREFACE

The strangest thing just happened. Troy called. Troy is my son—the only boy and oldest child in the sibling group my wife and I adopted. He and I haven't spoken meaningfully for maybe a dozen years or more, other than saying "Hi" at a couple of family functions. He left home when he was 17—he ran away from our house as soon as he was legally able—as two of his sisters would eventually do as well. He called because he had been following the work I've been doing on shame since I'd been posting some of it to Facebook.

He came to ask for help. Troy doesn't ask for help. He reminded me of that at lunch. He reminded me that he has too much pride to ask for help.

Help can be a four-letter word for people struggling with shame. The concept requires us to accept our humanity—that we are creatures in need. Accepting our neediness can be full of baggage as we have tried forever to prove to the world that we don't need anyone or anything, and acknowledging we are in need means acknowledging we are also weak and small in at least some areas. It also means acknowledging we simply can't make it on our own. Shame insists we must make it on our own. Pride is a defense mechanism shame uses to prevent us from acknowledging this weakness and asking for help.

Troy told me that for all of his 29 years, pride has been his ally— pride and anger. He said he used those things to fuel his will. He said he used his pride and anger to focus his energies to be able to "succeed" in life. To him, as with me, success often meant "not failing."

He remembered a story from youth group at our church when the youth group leader explained that pride was a bad thing. Troy remembered rejecting this idea at the time, but he was there at lunch that day to vanquish his pride and do what his pride insisted he didn't do: ask for help. He was there to ask for help because he no longer wanted anger to guide his path.

He spent the next hour and half telling me his story. He told me his story about wanting to be a better man. He would always pause, though, at the place many of us will pause to say "not that I'm a bad man"—but still stuck in the reality that he wasn't who he wanted to be. This struck me, as it's the sad reality of shame. Most of us aren't "bad" people. We hold jobs, raise kids, go to school, and contribute meaningfully to society in any number of ways. But we know we are not who we want to be and/or maybe we simply aren't living a life we want to live.

At 29 years old, Troy realized he was "in the grip of something," as he put it—he was in a battle with something inside himself. He thought he had been using that "something" to fuel his course, but he'd come to discover that maybe it had been using and manipulating him instead. He was not in control of it; it was in control of him. He was caught, alone, and could not see a way out. Through tears, he asked me to help him find a way out.

* * *

The main thing that has brought me peace in my journey is finding out that I am not alone. I'm not sure why that's of such vital importance, but what I do know is that the principal desire of "shame" is to separate us from ourselves and each other.

The first thing you might notice is how I address "shame." I don't treat it as an emotion, but rather I animate it—even giving it goals, objectives, and desires. I speak of shame as if it may be something outside ourselves or separate from us, which it is not—it is very much part of who we are—it is "us." Yet, it seemingly can have a different agenda than we may want for ourselves, as my own story suggests.

One of the ways—perhaps the main way—to fight against the effects of shame is to do what you can to prevent the alienation it desires. To that end, if I do nothing with this book but inform you that you are not alone, I have done significant damage to the forces of shame in the world. If you become aware that you are connected to me and every other being calling itself "human," then you have taken one significant step forward in the battle to retake your life from the influence of this destructive force.

That's why it's so important to tell our stories. "Shame keeps us from telling our own stories and prevents us from listening to others tell their stories" (Brown 2008, xxv). The *reason* for which is that shame's end game is separation. Although separation may prevent us from feeling the short-term pain of exposure, it is not a way of life. In fact, it may be *the* way of a slow, silent death.

Author Brené Brown, through her professional research on the subject, has concluded that shame is something we all have and that most of us

> *... if I do nothing with this book but inform you that you are not alone, I have done significant damage to the forces of shame in the world.*

are afraid to talk about. What we may not know is that the less we talk about it, the more it continues to exert control over our lives.

Because I'm increasingly tired of the control shame has over my life—the way I have to compete to win, always have to be right, suffer from chronic depression, and find myself constantly getting defensive whenever anyone dares question me—I will tell my story. As such, I'm about to do battle with this inner manipulator.

So, in this book, I tell my story. The goal of telling my story is not so that you can learn something unique from me (although you might). Shame is something people have been struggling with since biblical times, and countless books have been written on the subject. Besides, I think there is only limited value in facts and data and things that can be cognitively learned, as much as there is trans-formational value in the telling of a story.

> *It was clear from the data that we cannot give our children what we don't have.*

Instead, I hope you will learn you are not alone in this fight, which may embolden you to take up the fight as well. I mostly hope that for my kids. Brown convinced me of the importance of pursuing this cause when she said, "It was clear from the data that we cannot give our children what we don't have" (Brown, 2010, xi), and I want freedom for my children.

This won't be the last book on this subject. Shame will continue to retreat into the shadows when we fight back, only to resurface later in a different form or a different voice—a device folklore has come to term "shame-shifting." The battle is a lifelong struggle, so we need to continue to speak and listen with empathy and compassion.

Troy began telling me his story as soon as we said "hello," almost as if he intuitively knew it was the first necessary step toward freedom. The true lesson for me, however, would happen moments later. Troy was telling his story the way Troy talks—very loud and very animated. The entire place could have heard what was going on in the deep insides of his soul as he struggled to regain control of his life from his demons.

As we approached the counter at the sandwich shop to order our lunch (we hadn't even ordered yet), he only barely paused to tell the guy behind the counter what he wanted to eat. I was somewhat in shock and couldn't help but wonder what the guy making our subs thought about all this. His reply will stick with me forever:

"I know what you mean, man," he said to Troy. "I got the same stuff going on." He apologized for listening in, but said he couldn't help it. As Troy dared to share his story loud enough for the entire restaurant to hear, another human being found out he was not alone, and shame lost a little of its grip on all of us.

I hope this book encourages you in your own battle, as the writing of it has been an encouragement for me in mine. You can find additional resources and connect with me further at rickpattersonconnects.com.

We can never become resistant to shame; however, we can develop the resilience we need to recognize shame, move through it constructively and grow from our experiences (Brown 2008, xiv).

INTRODUCTION

Ten years ago . . . I named the core demon in my life. I named "shame." This means that I became aware of the massive destructive power shame had exerted in my life. I discovered that I had been bound by shame all my life. It ruled me like an addiction. I acted it out; I covered it up in subtle and not-so-subtle ways; I transferred it to my family, my clients, and the people I taught.

Shame was the unconscious demon I had never acknowledged. In becoming aware of the dynamics of shame, I came to see that shame is one of the major destructive forces in all human life. In naming shame I began to have power over it (Bradshaw 2005, xvii).

My hand was in a cast that Sunday morning as I took the pulpit. I had what's called a "boxer's fracture"—a break in the finger bone (typically the pinky) between the last knuckle and the wrist. It's called that because it frequently happens when someone strikes a hard object with a closed fist.

Whenever your hand is in a cast, you inevitably get the question, "What happened?" and I was dreading it. As a pastor, it was going to be hard to admit that I punched a door . . . then a wall . . . then a bookshelf . . . as I flew into a fit of rage because my teenage daughter, Tapricia, had rolled her eyes at me. My inner voice suggested I lie when people asked, or perhaps make up a grand illusion of saving the family from intruders. But there were too many witnesses. My daughters had seen my dark side; they didn't need to see me lie about it.

The most humiliating part was that the infraction was so small to elicit such a severe reaction. As I look back, I can see how petty the entire thing was. Who does that sort of thing? What was inside me that prompted such a violent reaction? How fortunate I was that I just hit those inanimate objects and not this little girl who had been entrusted to my care (I am her *adoptive* father)!

> *Why do we do the things we do and make decisions that we eventually regret?*

However, even as I type the words, I can see the lump in my hand now—10 years later—that the doctor said will always be there, serving as a reminder of this hidden driver inside.

To that end, the primary question this book asks is, "Why?" Why do we do the things we do and make decisions that we eventually regret? Why do we never do the things we really *want* to do? Why does my low self-esteem lock me up? Why am I so competitive that it ruins my relationships? Why must I hurt other people in order to feel good about myself? Why am I so consumed with my failures that I can't find a way to succeed anymore? Why am I so desperate for approval and praise that I'm willing to do things I don't want to do? And, by all means, why on earth do I bash my fist so hard into walls and bookshelves because a teenage girl—who I LOVE—rolls her eyes at me? By getting at the "why" we do what we do, we can begin to put together a plan to make changes that will allow us to re-own our lives and make the kinds of choices we can look back on with satisfaction.

The main thesis of this book is that the root cause of poor decisions is based deep inside our own psychology, in a place called "shame." That voice of shame has many different aliases, all of which fail to capture the real breadth and power it has: the enemy within, the inner saboteur, and the inner critic, to name a few. I believe that "shame" is what drives much of the poor decisions and behaviors that make it challenging to live our lives the way we want to live them.

This "thing" that causes us to lash out at others and ourselves (and frequently feel good about it), this "enemy within," can, without question, become a vehicle of death. It most certainly is capable of leading to our own demise if not also the demise of our fellow human beings. It is this inner reality, this toxin pumping through our veins, this self, and mutually destructive force that we must address before we do any more damage.

This book suggests that our hope for reducing the destructive tendencies we have toward ourselves and our fellow struggling humans is to understand this driver, this thing called shame, in order to put forth a plan for change—to reboot our internal drives so we can begin to function differently.

Many other books about "happiness" or "leading a more fulfilling life" get attention because they offer easy fixes. Believe me, I think it would be terrific if I could offer a simple, multistep program to shake the doldrums, pull ourselves up by our bootstraps, and get back in the game of enjoying life. I wish that plan existed because I would use it myself!

I offer no easy fix, and you should know that going in—but I offer you something better. I offer an invitation to a battle. I offer you an invitation to join me in the battle for our wills. I offer you an invitation to a battle to take back the rightful control of your life from decisions that have been harming you and the ones you love. This is an invitation to live the life of freedom that you've so long hoped for and desired.

I dedicate this book to my adopted children—Troy, Tilonda, TiShanté, and Tapricia—who have survived the onslaught of shame on many levels. I specify they were adopted because this itself brings with it a certain degree of shame induction. They are also African American. I have been educated (by them) about these challenges. Finally, three are women—a gender in many cultures around the world that suffers its own realm of shame.

> **The goal is to expose the way shame manipulates our ability to make effective and healthy decisions**

Although my doctoral dissertation was on how shame motivates and manipulates our lives, it's been my children who have taught me a great deal about how debilitating shame can be, how early it enters our lives, and the sheer, lifelong determination involved in rewriting the script you were handed. They have helped me coauthor this book through their stories, inspiration, and my own desire to help them see themselves as the warriors they are. I hope to give them some freedom from what has haunted me.

This book offers some of their story combined with examples from my own life—from my time as a parent as well as my time in professional ministry and my years in corporate America—to help us explore the origins of anger, depression, anxiety, fear, low self-esteem, and insatiable egotism. Once we know their source—their principal drivers—we can prepare a game plan to deal with this condition plaguing not only us but our families, friends, and coworkers.

The goal is to expose the way shame manipulates our ability to make effective and healthy decisions—as I've seen played out in my own life, the lives of my children, and the lives of my coworkers in ministry and the business community.

Finally, the book concludes with lessons from all these experiences that have given me a fresh set of eyes on how to deal with this problem. I give some hope for our ability to begin the process of making better choices and not letting our emotions and psychology make our decisions for us. I show how we can have more empathy, more compassion, and more integrity in our lives, which will hopefully allow us to release some of the resentment, anger, defeatism, and triumphalism that has been fueling our life this far.

When you're finished reading this book, you will have acquired some language so you can begin to:

- **STOP some of the behaviors you participate in to shame yourself and, sadly, shame others, which frequently makes us feel temporarily good about ourselves.**
- **STOP being manipulated by your defense mechanisms like perfectionism and your need for admiration.**
- **START being more empathetic and caring toward yourself and others.**
- **START being able to accomplish the tasks—large and small—that your inner critic has been demanding you are not prepared to handle.**

I can guarantee you—here, already in the first words of this book—that the voice of shame, that voice that attempts to convince me I am less than I really am, will be my companion as I attempt to get these ideas down on paper. That voice that says the ideas themselves are "stupid" stands ready to make its case every time I pause.

That voice that reminds me that no one will care about my positions on these issues is pulling up a chair beside me even now, suggesting I'm not qualified to write on this subject. That voice that says I will fail, I will have wasted my time, and that I will have embarrassed myself in the process is calling for me to pay it some attention. That voice, inside my own being, has one goal: to silence me. Its goal is to stop me from helping myself and, potentially, from helping others in the process.

As you read this, I hope you find a voice that reminds you that you are not alone in this battle. I hope you find a traveling partner in your journey who encourages you to overcome your fear. I hope you and I both find a way to walk away from the control shame has over our lives. This book is my attempt to practice what I preach. I hope you'll join me.

CHAPTER 1

You Love Me,
You Love Me Not?

"I'm the ugly one..."
—Tilonda McGuffey

I can't remember if we had already adopted the kids or if maybe we were still foster parenting them when my eldest daughter gave me the story of a lifetime. I do remember the floral print sofa that was the first couch my wife and I bought after getting married. It would later meet its demise when our Great Dane, Melody, would camp there for the night after being sprayed by a skunk.

The sofa was against the east wall of the house, sitting between the two tower speakers that were all the rage in the '80s, and it was set perpendicular to the sliding glass doors leading to our back yard.

I was coming through those doors to experience something that would change my outlook forever.

As I came through the doors heading into the house, my mind was certainly preoccupied with whatever was happening in the field that day as I was just beginning to raise cattle. I passed by the couch where Tilonda, my eldest daughter, was sitting. She was in the middle of the couch fidgeting with her hair as young girls tend to do, and probably waiting for me to come in. She announced to me with no particular fanfare and with a little smile that she was "the ugly one."

Now, whatever was in my mind was immediately replaced with this statement from my daughter. I had never been a father before welcoming these sisters and their brother into my home, so I was not schooled in the finer elements of child-induced speechlessness, but evidently had instinct enough to know that whatever was about to happen needed my undivided attention. I wasn't there to fix, I was there to listen. That's harder than it seems in a moment like this because we want to fix.

Fixing is for us as much as it is for the other. Fixing helps us feel good about ourselves—that we have accomplished something. Frequently, if we can't "fix," we feel bad and maybe even make the other person feel bad as well because they are un-fixable. Listening is hard because it requires us to shelve our own issues to simply focus on another human being.

As my daughter described her ugliness, I immediately believed I knew where she was headed (another good reason we should listen more is because our ego/shame insists we always know where people are headed). In our culture, we all know how female beauty is defined and, somehow, by elementary school, she too, was aware—unambiguously aware, evidently. Still, I didn't want to assume I knew what was going on—I certainly didn't want to put thoughts in her heart that weren't already there.

"What do you mean?" I asked, as if a seasoned pro at parenting.

She said, "Compared to my sisters . . . I'm the ugly one."

Images of her sisters quickly ran through my mind and I began to have some internal confirmation that I knew where she was headed. All the kids we adopted were biological siblings—three sisters and a brother. They all had the same mom but different dads. The younger two sisters had the same father who had somehow engendered them with more "Caucasian" features, although they were all black.

I asked my daughter again, "What do you mean?" I think I was now sitting beside her. Then she hit me with it. Even though I saw it coming, I wasn't ready. "Because my nose is wider, and my lips are bigger. Because my skin is darker and my hair is kinkier." She was still twisting her hair and smiling. She didn't seem at all hurt by the idea. It was said in such a plain, matter-of-fact way; it's as if she wanted to inform me she had a loose tooth.

I was in shock, although I don't think my face gave me away. In a moment that seemed like hours, I tried to understand how this had been communicated to a girl who was this young still. I can't imagine anyone said it to her outright, but I suppose anything was possible. That said, you also don't have to look beyond the media to see how feminine beauty is defined in our culture. All I could think was: who stole my little girl . . .

I can't remember what I said in that moment. I remember thinking it probably didn't matter what I said. What mattered is that I had a lifetime of work ahead of me rewriting the script that had been handed to her. "Rewriting the script" is probably the wrong phrase— rewriting a script is probably not humanly possible. My goal was to propose an alternative narrative. I began to call her "Beautiful"—a name she has since tattooed inside her right bicep.

With as much horror as that situation could fill me, it still paled in comparison to what was happening inside her. She loved giving and getting hugs but, as the hug began, she would push back, separating our torsos. She was unable to make eye contact in those moments, although she seemed skilled at eye contact when talking about very serious and not-so-serious issues. She confessed one day, when she was about the same age, that she had decided not to feel things any more. How can a child that young articulate such thoughts?

What she couldn't yet articulate was the sense of worthlessness that comes from being abandoned to one degree or another by her grandmother, her mother, a legal father, and a biological father. What does that do to a little girl who already doesn't physically "look beautiful"? It likely makes you abandon a desire to feel because, I imagine, "feeling" is a rather painful experience.

Oddly, when I tell this story in my public speaking seminars, I am able to show a picture of her and, without exception, people are shocked at how physically beautiful she actually is. It's a very hard thing to explain when you look at someone that beautiful how they could consider themselves to be the ugly one. Perhaps it's how anorexics feel fat? I don't know.

> *How any one thing has the ability to take what is so obviously true and make us believe the opposite gives us an indication of the power of this enemy inside us.*

Regardless of what she has since tattooed on her arm, I knew her life would be a struggle—because of the shame she carried inside. There was going to be no quick fix for this script that she had inscribed on her soul. I knew her inner voice would continually be reminding her she was ugly and worthy of abandonment; all you have to do to see the abject power of shame is take one look at the physical beauty of my daughter who believes and acts upon the belief that she's ugly. How any one thing has the ability to take what is so obviously true and make us believe the opposite gives us an indication of the power of this enemy inside us.

Tilonda needed to have her obvious beauty validated, though. I don't know if this is true of all people or all girls, but the more I speak with women, the more I see how prevalent it is. Beyond that, however, and seemingly contradictory to the first issue, she seemed drawn to men who would physically abuse her. She also seemed to hope, at times, to actually entice people to physically abuse her. She certainly tried that with me.

It was in middle school that the challenges escalated, as they always seem to do. She had snuck out of the house with some "banned" clothing in her gym bag, intent on changing into them when she got to school. Clothing, it seems to me, is another sign of the shame we carry. Anything that screams "look at me" is a result of the need we have for some sort of affirmation that we're worth looking at—and my daughter, along with many girls her age (and men my age, I reckon), certainly had that need.

She was discovered and lost basketball practice for the night as a consequence. On the way home, she flew into a fit of rage, using her legs to push the driver's seat I was in, and me as a result, up into the steering wheel of the moving car that was taking us home. I repositioned the kids so she was now riding in the front seat beside me when she began to kick me and proceeded to kick the gear shifter of our moving car from drive into reverse.

After pulling over, I suggested that she just let her anger go. I suggested I was there to take it. She began to beat my head with her fists until her hands hurt too much to continue. The dust then settled. She was out of breath. Her siblings were in something of shock. Me . . . well, I was in disbelief but glad the encounter seemed to be drawing to a close.

My wife came down to pick us all up. Tilonda sat quietly in the back of the car as my wife closed up shop at the elementary school where she is the principal. As we sat there in the dark—me in the front of the suburban and her in the very back seat with an entirely empty seat between us—I heard her quiet voice ask, "Do you hate me?"

That is the question lurking in her soul to this day. I believe: "Do you hate me?" That is the question that motivated much of her behavior. Perhaps it is the key question shame asks. Many scholars

> *"Do you hate me?"*
> *Perhaps it is the key*
> *question shame asks.*

have said shame is related to a primary fear of abandonment—of not being connected to other human beings. Being a "hateful" human yourself will certainly ensure you are left alone, forever.

Then she asked the follow-up, "Why didn't you hit me back? I would have hit me back."

Looking back, this daughter, Tilonda, had been unable in this instance to hit my shame trigger the way her younger sister did when she rolled her eyes at me, even though her younger sister may have been processing that very same question, consciously or subconsciously. The situation with Tilonda certainly was more aggressive and damaging, but I wasn't psychologically threatened by it. She didn't roll her eyes. She struck me with her fists. That will never hurt me.

In the case of Tapricia, who rolled her eyes but never physically touched me, she was able to strike my own sense of self-hate. I almost did strike another human being in a shameful rage that day—and it was my own daughter. I would have forever emboldened in her a greater sense of her value—that she was worthy of being struck by a grown man. How is such a thing possible? Whenever I am tempted to think that this force called shame doesn't have a capacity for evil, I remember that moment.

Shame has also been called the fear of disconnection. If this is the case, then there is a very fine line between the questions "Do you hate me?" and "Will you leave me?" It also doesn't take much of a stretch of the imagination to see how a young girl who had been abandoned so early in life to become a ward of the state might harbor some shame that she was worthy of such a fate later in life as well.

As with all humanity, my kids still struggle. Evidently, all of Tilonda's boyfriends have not been able to overcome her sense of inadequacy. It seems likely that she may still wonder if, *today, in this moment*, I love her or hate her. She may wonder if *today* I think she's still beautiful even though I told her *yesterday* she is. There is no tattoo for overcoming that, and attempting to convince someone they shouldn't feel what they feel can frequently backfire.

> *How can we enable an individual to work through a core be-*
> *lief of not being good enough as a person, to emerge from an*
> *imprisoning identity infused with doubt, shame, and fear to*
> *one that's freeing? Attempts at either ignoring these core beliefs,*
> *convincing him otherwise, or trying to rid the person of them*
> *backfire. Such attempts deny the reality of those feelings and*
> *thereby engender shame about having them in the first place*
> (Kaufman 1992, 138).

SHAME AND THE ART OF SELF-DEFENSE

> *"It is instilled in thousands of American males from an early*
> *age that one of their requirements is to be able to both dish*
> *out and take a lot of pain. They are taught the rules of this*
> *road in gyms, rings, backyards and fields all over America."*
> — Henry Rollins (2013)

It's always interesting to compare who you were as a child with who you've become as an adult. When I was getting my doctoral degree, I asked my mom what kind of kid I was growing up. She said I was quiet and thoughtful, a **dreamer**. I was very sensitive, introverted, and introspective; I thought about myself and how I fit into things all the time. These are all things I vividly remember about myself but are things people today may not see much of in me anymore.

I quickly learned to categorize those things as "not good" and decided I would have to go about being broken of them in order to get ready for what the world would require. Little did I know that "there is no more disastrous path than to seek to violate one's basic nature. If an introverted individual feels deficient because of that introvertedness and seeks to become extroverted, *as though this were the better way to be*, the seeds of neurosis are already growing" (Kaufman 1992, 151).

I saw in school how "popular" and "accepted" were defined. Those goals of youth, being popular and accepted, didn't typically belong to the kind/thoughtful kid, but rather to the thoughtless/mean kid. I never found value, as a kid, being the one who was sensitive and liked to think. However, I am fairly confident I saw value being ascribed to those who weren't this way. It wasn't the poets who were admired by their peers at that age!

I was born an idealist. Maybe all kids are. I was born sensitive, quiet, artistic, and relational. If you were to ask people around me in my adult life to describe me, this is very much *not* the description they would offer. Very early in life, I realized how I was wired was a tough combination and would make survival a challenge. People inflicted pain—not just on me but on each other—and I almost couldn't bear to watch it any longer.

> *The lie is that not being enough is a bad thing and that we must be about fixing that issue.*

I remember confessing to my parents my dislike for people and my dream of becoming a mountain man (Grizzly Adams was my hero). I dreamed of escaping to the mountain country with a bear, a mule, and a cantankerous old flapjack–making man (I was crushed to later see images of actor Dan Haggerty arrested for drug trafficking). So clear was my disdain for humanity, my mother would later object to the idea of me becoming a pastor, keenly aware of my aversion to people.

Side note: Hopefully you can see shame creeping in to my own normal, Caucasian, middle-class life here as well. Remember that the chief goal of shame is to separate and by my early years I already wanted to head for the hills!

I learned early that being "me" was not a good way to go through life—that I was "not enough." I've come to believe that this is the case for all humanity to one extent or another. This is our common heritage. As my Dutch friend said to me, "We've all been hit by the same windmill."

I also believe that the lie itself is *not* that you are not enough. No one is ever enough. That's part of being human. *The lie is that not being enough is a bad thing and that we must be about fixing that issue.* If you pick that lie up at any point, for any reason, at any age, you're likely to be living under the curse of that lie and that curse has a name: shame.

That lie creates anxiety, legalism, rage, and overachievement—among a whole host of other symptoms and defense strategies this book is not large enough to contain. It results in reactions ranging from a passion to accomplish in order to prove to the world you are of value or a shrinking from any responsibility or "presence" in order to avoid being discovered for who you are. All of which works great—until it stops working.

Because it would be a good long wait between childhood and mountain man-hood, I would have to find a way to cope with my fear of being exposed. I would live into the system rather than fight against it—I would become productive. Success, or perhaps "safety," seemed to me to be defined by one's ability to exercise power over your circumstances—including the people around you. This would be the transition that lay ahead of me as I began to create what is frequently termed my "false self."

While my shift to pragmatism and productivity appeared almost predetermined at that point, I've come to see a move across town in fourth grade as sealing its inevitability. It was a total life shift that would strip me of any illusion of safety in my surroundings. The meaningful friendships I had were torn away, and I would have to "earn" new ones. Never before had this aspect of relationships been so real to me.

What would there be about me that would draw people who already had friends? I'd need to figure it out in order to compete. I knew it wouldn't be looks, an outgoing personality, or profound athleticism! It was at this time that I became completely aware that I had nothing to offer except sensitivity, thoughtfulness, and intro-spection and that I was about to be gutted on the fields of flag foot-ball, marbles, and at the game affectionately referred to as "smear the queer." At the time, I don't think "queer" had any relationship to being gay, at least I don't remember it as such. What I do remember is that the game took a skill set I had yet to develop.

Throughout grade school, these issues concretized; I still didn't have much to offer and was quite often simply alone. Relationships went from being spontaneous and joyful to utilitarian, their value extending only as far as what they were able to give me. This, of course, mirrored my understanding that my value was also deter-mined by what I could produce for others.

I was smart and observant, which, in and of itself, wouldn't matter for some time because, as we all know, smart is of no productive "value" at that age. However, I would watch and learn what worked and what didn't. I would learn to discern who had something to offer me and how I could offer something to others. This mindset would be affirmed when I entered the church and corporate America years later and would become the basis for all my shame-based defenses.

My oldest daughter—the one who had declared herself the ugly one—put things this way when I was out to breakfast with her recently.

She described how "regulars" who come into the restaurant where she waitresses react to her—they love her smile! They are always impressed with the way she seems to embrace life and seems so alive. Her smile, people say, is contagious—which it is. She said, "people don't know *me* Rick—they don't know the struggle or what's going on inside."

What they are seeing is what she is projecting for the world to see. She is projecting what she thinks they probably want to see. She's projecting what psychologists call the "false self" and hiding what they call the "true self." What she's showing the world is what Eve put on to prevent people from seeing her "naked" all the way back in the Garden of Eden—fig leaves.

Psychologists have written endlessly about the "false self," especially when it comes to the issue of hiding shame. John Bradshaw has said, "Toxic shame is unbearable and always necessitates a cover-up, a false self. Since one feels his true self is defective and flawed, one needs a false self that is not" (Bradshaw 2005, xvii). What's remarkable about it is how person after person I meet is doing the exact same thing.

Like my daughter, I was creating my false self by observing what was necessary to survive and then clothing myself with it. This persona is "what most people want from you and reward you for, and what you choose to identify with, for some reason" (Rohr 2011, 128). The problem is, "your self image is not substantial or lasting; it is just created out of your own mind, desire, and choice – and everybody else's preferences for you!" (Rohr 2011, 129).

WELCOME TO THE GRAND ILLUSION

Productivity, for me, was a defense mechanism that prevented the exposure of my "not enoughness" to the world. It was the proverbial fig leaf I was hiding behind to prevent my nakedness from being exposed to the world. It is the thing my eldest daughter wears to work—something most of us wear to work, or church, or wherever we fear exposure.

I became someone I wasn't to sustain myself, physically and psychologically. By the time I hit corporate America, I was fully living into the curse—the development of my false self was now in full swing and full control. I had completely set aside what it meant to be "me" to become what the world said I needed to be.

I set aside feelings for decision making—making decisions is

Productivity, for me, was a defense mechanism that prevented the exposure of my "not enoughness" to the world.

harder to do with feelings. I twisted self-awareness into self-centeredness. I traded meekness for power. And it worked! The world affirmed my choice to abandon myself and become someone else. I was getting promotions, money, praise, and recognition. I finally was someone; I just wasn't me. Eventually, however, with any luck this charade will run aground.

> *It is one of the turning points in therapy when the patient comes to the emotional insight that all the love she has captured with so much effort and self-denial was not meant for her as she really was, that the admiration for her beauty and achievements was aimed at this beauty and achievements and not the child herself. In therapy, the small and lonely child that is hidden behind her achievements wakes up and asks: "What would have happened if I appeared before you sad, needy, angry, furious? . . . Does this mean it was not me you loved, but only what I pretended to be?"* (Miller 1997, 5).

Corporate America still fascinates me as I look back on my *first* 12 years there. It is one place that honestly conveys the truth of life. It is a great system for rewarding productivity, although it can confuse actually productive people with people who are just plain lucky. There are raises, promotions, and meaning placed on you for your accomplishments and, much like the sports world, there's no pretending that value is derived from any other source than your win/loss column.

It still shocks me when I hear people complain that they gave their best 20 years to "this or that" company only to be discarded when no longer needed. In my experience in corporate America, this was never a hidden reality—this should take no one as a surprise. People who are upset with "the company" for turning their back on them after they lose their contributiveness have that institution confused with their mother.

Corporate America never pretended value was located in anything other than what you are able to produce and for that—its integrity—it should be applauded. I fell in love with the integrity of the whole process, it was honest—perhaps one of the few honest relationships I'd had. I've returned to corporate America after 10 years in ministry and have found the same principles at play, maybe even increasingly so. It's not about "who you are" but "what you can do."

I found myself sucked into a similar spiral with the church. I seemed to experience value being conferred based on the number of committees on which you served, how frequently and regularly you attended worship, how many visits you made to the elderly, or, the biggest one of all, how many people you were able to invite to and retain in the religious system. I'm open to the idea that I was just projecting my world view onto the church at the time. That's what we do when we are unaware we are living in an illusion—it becomes our reality for every circumstance.

As a result, I pursued a more corporate relationship with the church that was also based on performance. That way, I would be able to measure God's acceptance of me and would be able to compete with all the people God must certainly have to choose between. Perhaps I might even gain God's favor and I would attempt to measure this through the favor I might curry with the institutional church.

Even now, it strikes me as odd that I led a congregation of people in a denomination that insists we are unable to earn God's favor, yet it was the only thing I probably really cared about. However, I was not alone in my drive for results.

I had learned early God wanted us "to be *both* faithful and fruitful." I learned "Jesus has given the church a job to do. We will either succeed or fail at it. Using this definition, every church should want to be successful! What is the alternative? . . . Failure." Faithfulness would be defined as "accomplishing as much as possible with the resources and talents God has given" us (Warren 1995, 65).

What if I failed? I wasn't about to find out. I was going to accomplish for Christ. I would *not* be a failure. Productivity was a system that served me well to this point in my life; I saw no reason to give it up now.

The survival of local congregations and denominations (as in corporate America), can appear to rely on people like me—driven by our inner shame to produce and contribute, particularly in regard to getting more people in the pews and more sales in the register. My father once described the similarity between a Rotary meeting and a church meeting: both spending huge amounts of time "in great hand wringing about how to get more people to join them." Churches living in fear of failure in a religious system whose most frequent command is "fear not."

In the church, I saw I was being affirmed and loved for my ability to teach and to see things differently. I decided to head off to seminary to get the training required to "pontificate," as my father would say of people who insisted on driveling on and on about issues without having any real impact. By the way, that concept of pontification is actually biblical. Paul says that you can be the best public speaker in the world but if you don't have love, you are a resounding gong or a clanging symbol. I believe that was at the heart of my father's "pontification" remarks.

I was a really good preacher. I still am. Today I wonder how much of it was gong clanging. At the time, I had not love, but I had a deep inner need to be important and to prove myself. Perhaps that's the opposite of love, I'm not sure. My goal was to save the world through my pronouncements not so much for purposes of saving the world (that might be based in love) but for purposes of being adored by the masses because I was so smart, had such amazing visionary leadership, and was such a good communicator. I owed my greatness to serve the masses, I suppose.

I am reminded here of my buddy who asked why I entered ministry and wanted to start a church. My response was "because I couldn't find a good one," and that I could do it better than what was out there. Ironically, my call to ministry had nothing to do with my love for people, my desire to serve, or any other Christian tenet. It only had to do with my desire to pontificate and be recognized for my pontifications.

> *At least I knew that even those chosen by Jesus as his first disciples experienced the same crisis of shame and need for recognition.*

I also recall the story of the two disciples who argued about which of them would be the greatest and who would sit at Jesus' right hand and who would sit on the left. Who would be the greatest among them? At least I know I was in good company with my need to be great. At least I knew that even those chosen by Jesus as his first disciples experienced the same crisis of shame and need for recognition. At least I knew I was not alone. The problem was Jesus' response, which is perhaps the great indelible truth of the Christian religion: **the least shall be greatest, the last shall be first.**

At any rate, I now had two institutions that seemed to love my productivity: corporate America and the church. My wife made deciding which to follow easy. We would *not* be taking any corporate transfers, which would forever limit the job opportunities I'd have in the business world. So, knowing my corporate productivity would become limited, and there would be others more productive and sacrificial than me, I decided to invest in the church. Besides, wasn't pleasing God an even greater challenge with even greater heights of potential value?

It's hard to write this. It's hard to acknowledge these realities publically. I hold no ill will toward either institution, the church or corporate America. **My problem was not the institutions**, my problem was inside of me. "My immediate problem [was] me and the silent conspiracy I have had with the institution – the conspiracy that allowed that institution to rule my life" (Palmer 1997, 170). I'd sold my soul to gain the world, and it was all an illusion. I speak these things in hopes that by acknowledging reality and the power of the shame drive inside me, I can break the bonds I have with institutions. I also speak these things to let others know that they are not alone.

Lynne Hybels helped me see I was not alone as she reflected on how the myth of productivity, improperly controlled, had perpetuated in human lives during one of the greatest church plants in history—the 15,000-member Willow Creek Community Church.

> *The dream had been not just to build a church, but to build it together . . . first to die was the sense of community . . . as the pace increased, the intimacy decreased . . . divorce followed on the heels of several staff resignations and lay leader departures . . . our sacrifice exceeded God's demand . . . and so two by two we paid the price in our marriages . . . Bill and I look back at these years with deep sadness and regret . . . **Bill's understanding of his own addiction to fruitbearing would have served him and the entire core group so well back then . . .** (Hybels 1995, 85 [emphasis added]).*

The Hybels learned what I, too, would have to experience: fruitbearing and "productivity" were an illusion, generated by shame intent on propping up my weak self-image. I am not the first to have discovered that the church was not immune to such things. However, it would be a long road to get me to those realizations.

SHAME MAY BE DRIVING THE BUS, BUT OUR FEAR OF PAIN CHARTS THE COURSE

We have to ask ourselves: What gets us into a situation where we need to live in a grand illusion, anyway? What makes us generate false selves and compile these defense mechanisms?

Tony Robbins has made the pain/pleasure formula of motivation famous, and I applaud it, myself. He contends that all human actions are motivated by a desire to either seek pleasure or avoid pain, with the avoidance of pain being up to four times as powerful as a means of directing our path. Because shame is such a powerfully painful experience in our lives, it's little wonder that we've developed defense mechanisms to prevent ourselves from experiencing it.

The first thing we do out of fear of experiencing pain is establish in ourselves a voice—probably a familiar voice—perhaps a co-mingling of our own with a parent or particular authority figure from our past. This voice we commonly have come to know as our inner critic is our earliest defense mechanism against pain.

My inner critic has been my constant companion in all of life's adventures, including authoring this book. The closer I get to the finish line of this, the more my inner voice insists I

> *This voice we commonly have come to know as our inner critic is our earliest defense mechanism against pain.*

shut down the computer and hang it up. I wish things were going the other way. I wish I were gaining courage and feeling freer about the entire thing, but I'm not. As I get close to the finish line, that inner critic has decided to take a different approach, realizing it can't stop me from writing. It is now insisting that I do it perfectly and that I not publish this work until it's perfect. My fear of pain is attempting to chart my course.

At first blush, we can chastise that inner voice and tell it to shut up and we can move on with making our own decisions and being successful. However, it's probably best to pause right here and understand that your inner voice (i.e., *you*) is just trying to protect you from pain. My inner voice doesn't want me to experience the pain of having my ideas rejected. My inner voice doesn't want to experience the pain of exposure I will feel when I confess my "not enoughness" to the world. My inner critic is simply trying to prevent me from being misunderstood or, God forbid, from getting busted for failing to punctuate properly!

We all have this inner voice, our inner critic. But, following the most important rule we have, we must not just ask ourselves *how* that voice got there but *why* it's there—especially when it seems so *self*-destructive. I am suggesting that it's there, at least initially, for your own defense.

This inner voice we hear is just trying to do us some favors early on. It's funny to think how an inner critic is something that best serves our self-defense but it does—or for such we created it. The function of your inner critic is to prevent you from doing potentially embarrassing things (like writing a book on shame), so as to help you forego the pain you will experience if and when the book is rejected and sitting by the hundreds in boxes in your basement.

Your inner critic is literally attempting to protect you from *you*. It stops you from truly living your own life for fear that you will be shown for who you really are. Perhaps you will fail. Perhaps you will do something the world might believe to be stupid. Perhaps

> *...we must not just ask ourselves how that voice got there but why it's there.*

you will be laughed at or otherwise persecuted. Your inner critic was born out of your need to keep that from happening. It was created to minimize the amount of pain you would feel. And it probably played a very helpful role in helping you survive middle school, a difficult upbringing, dating, a disability, or any number of challenging life experiences.

If you were about to go out on a limb, the voice would simply say, "Don't be an idiot." If you went anyway and the limb broke, that voice would say, "You idiot—why didn't you listen to me?" What's odd about the voice is that it's still you. You are having an argument with a very real entity that is still actually you! It's weird.

There's an important distinction I want to make here that I will expand on later in the book. Going out on a limb may be a bad idea. It may even be a dumb thing to do. However, your inner critic won't say "don't do that dumb thing," it will say "don't be an idiot." Your inner critic

> *Your inner critic will attempt to connect who you are as a person with specific mistakes you've made.*

will attempt to connect who you are as a person with specific mistakes you've made. Such that if you *do* something dumb that means you *are* something dumb. If your inner critic can convince you that if you fail you are a failure, the odds that it will get your attention increase dramatically.

That inner critic also becomes helpful as we develop more specific, outward-focused defense strategies to help prevent our soft insides from being exposed to the world seeking to destroy them. For example, it's integral in helping us develop our false self that we project to the world. It also helps you see who to manipulate and when to manipulate them in order to achieve your goals. It urges you on to maximize your productivity and prevent your "laziness," *so the world won't find out who you really are.*

It certainly reminds you that you need to be perfect. **It will never tell you *why* you need to be perfect or productive**, other than to remind you that people are watching, and that's all that matters.

Richard Rohr does a masterful job in his book *Falling Upward* of describing this inner being as the "loyal soldier" that "gets us through the first half of life safely" but also warns that the loyal soldier "gives you so much security and validation that you may confuse his voice with the very voice of God." He says, "If this inner voice has kept you safe for many years as your inner voice of authority, you may end up not being able to hear the real voice of God. The loyal soldier is the voice of all your early authority figures. His or her ability to offer shame, guilt, warnings, boundaries, and self doubt is the gift that never stops giving" (Rohr 2011, 43).

The goal of this inner voice is intended to keep you from harm—to keep you from making mistakes that will cause you pain (usually emotional pain). Eventually, as Rohr argues, it is time to grow up to live your own life, make your own decisions, and, quite possibly, make your own mistakes.

You Need to Make Your Own Mistakes

The challenge of this book is to embrace what it means to be human: to make mistakes and to struggle daily with our limitations. This book is not intended to help you overcome your limitations because doing so would be an illusion. If you are human, you will always have limitations. However, we also have to make sure we are making *our own* mistakes by making our *own decisions* and not ones being dictated to us by some inner voice attempting to help protect us from the fact that we are just human after all. The key is knowing *why* we are making the decisions we are making.

> "If I had to go back and say, 'what would you change?,' I would probably go back and follow John Madden's and Bill Parcells' advice to me, and that was make your own mistakes, don't make someone else's," Millen said in the film. "John would say to me all the time, 'Your name's on the top of the list. You make a decision, make sure it's your decision.'"—Matt Millen,

reflecting on his failed tenure as the general manager of the National Football League's Detroit Lions (Rogers 2013)

As I mentioned in the introduction, there's a voice welling up in my soul reminding me of my lack of qualifications to write on this or any subject. Perhaps you are familiar with that voice in your own spirit. This voice, as I've argued, is philosophically trying to look out for my own good. It's trying to prevent you from feeling the pain of vulnerability and rejection. That may have been what I needed when I was a child. I am now an adult. The goal of this book is to disarm that critic so the choices we make are our own choices and not the choices of some voice in our head that conflicts with everything else we know to be true about ourselves. Our goal is to free ourselves to make our own mistakes and not the mistakes of any other voice crying to us out of fear or shame.

In the quote from Matt Millen, he's discussing how his draft choices were overly influenced by others. Matt was describing that he didn't make his own mistakes; he didn't draft the players out of college he wanted to draft but took too much advice from others. I suggest Matt was hearing the same voice I hear in myself. Even though the entire Detroit Lion's agency was paying *him* to make those choices, trusting *him* to make those decisions because *they* believed in *him*, he didn't trust himself. That inner critic was reminding him that he didn't belong in the front office even though an entire NFL franchise disagreed.

It has been argued that this was yet another opportunity for Millen to shift blame for his choices to someone else—to not take responsibility for the Lions having the worst record in history with him at the helm. Millen is quite clear in his interviews that he is responsible for his choices and his mistakes. The point of his statement was not to shift blame to other people and their mistakes, but rather to own his own regret that he gave them too much credence out of the fear of making his own decisions.

This is an interesting argument, though. If we allow other

things—people, forces, whatever—to make our decisions for us, we won't be to blame for them. Blame can then lie elsewhere. Blame is a frequent shame-based defense mechanism and a weapon that your inner critic will quickly hand you when you get backed into a corner. However, it's a lie.

This argument that shame is driving our decisions is not intended to let us personally off the hook for our bad choices under some "the devil made me do it" cliché. That inner critic, the shame we carry, is every bit us—and we are it. If we pay it heed, the decisions we make are still entirely our own for which we will be held responsible. Just ask Matt Millen or my kids! Our goal is to regain the choices for ourselves that we have handed over to our psychology to make on our behalf.

> *This argument that shame is driving our decisions is not intended to let us personally off the hook for our bad choices under some "the devil made me do it" cliché.*

A month or so after I had broken my hand, my middle daughter, TiShanté, was chastising her younger sister for enticing me to smash my hand to bits by rolling her eyes. TiShanté wanted to blame Tapricia for her role in the event, as if to say it was all her fault. Tapricia simply replied, "That was his choice."

That was a message we had attempted to forge into all of them at the youngest of age: **we are the only ones responsible for our actions.** She reminded her sister that it was my choice to smash up my hand and that we are all responsible for our choices in life. As much as I wanted her to shoulder some of the blame for my actions, she refused. We taught her well . . .

I had to deal with the power of the eye roll—that was my responsibility. The eye roll is a skill we have developed—a weapon, developed by teenage children, girls mostly—to inflict damage where damage can be done: the psyche. A teenage girl knows she most likely cannot inflict physical damage on me, although my daughters have tried. The eye roll, however, on the shamed psyche, cuts deep and is virtually indefensible.

What the eye roll says is, "You are stupid." The eye roll finds you in that place of great infantile sensitivity, and there is no defense for it. If we didn't think there was the possibility that this teenage girl was right, it wouldn't affect us so dramatically. The worse we feel about ourselves, the more dramatically the eye roll will affect us.

Several years later, I was sitting in a room of congregants who had issues with the way the church was conducting business. There were two guys there—friends of mine—who had been raising concerns and issues prior to this meeting being called. In my mind, they were questioning my positions on things and my leadership capabilities. They were questioning things I feared about myself to be true but that, in my defensiveness, I may not have been able to hear.

I had spoken with them separately about the issue at lunch a couple weeks earlier. They said they had no issue. They said they used to have an issue, but that they'd let it go. I challenged them on this. Had they let it go? Did they still question foundational principles of this ministry? Would they be talking about it with other people in other venues? They assured me things were fine.

In this meeting, I brought up some of the rationale for why I do what I do—I brought up some of the bases for the ministry. One of the guys was across the room and, as I spoke, he unleashed the weapon. He looked at the other guy, who was sitting next to me, and rolled his eyes. It found me in that exact same place it did when my daughter did it to me and I reacted the exact same way.

Without hesitation, I said in a loud and clear voice, "F#$x you!" then looking at the other guy sitting next to me—just to be clear, I guess—I said, "and F#$x you, too." The room fell silent. I'm pretty sure that's not how Jesus would have handled it and probably not what people were expecting from their pastor, or a friend, or anyone in their right mind. I resigned the next day. Like the lump in my hand, that lump is still there as well, and I haven't pastored since. This is an affliction that finds us all, **from parents and pastors to Playboy Playmates.**

> *Our whole being is nothing but a fight against the dark forces within ourselves. To live is to war with trolls in the heart and soul.* — Henrik Ibsen

As I write this, there's another person reeling from the repercussions of her own choices splashed all over the headlines.

A *Playboy* Playmate of the Year photographed an unsuspecting and unaware lady who was changing in the locker room of her gym and posted it to social media with the caption, "If I can't unsee this, neither can you." Her face and body—the face and body of modern American beauty—was placed conveniently in the foreground so we could get a direct comparison between her and her unsuspecting victim, someone not as slim, young, or fit as this Playmate.

She later expressed regret for making the post. Giving her the benefit of the doubt that she actually regretted making that decision, the question then is *why* she felt it necessary to do the act at all. What was driving her decision to act in a manner that not only brought harm to another human being, but was also *self*-destructive in the process? In fact, that's what she herself would later tweet: that she needed to understand why she would do such a thing.

There is something in all of us pushing us to make decisions we later regret. There are voices we hear. Sometimes we have a chance to process those voices and to make a better decision for ourselves and those around us, and sometimes we just act, only to be horrified by the result. Those voices, those hidden influences, all come from a place I call *shame.*

Shame has a way of goading us into punching walls, shouting down our children, and belittling people we don't even know and many we do. It has a way of controlling the decisions we make at work or at home based on our fears of what other people might think of us. Shame has a way of causing us to lash out in violence or recoil in scared voicelessness. Shame is the great manipulator of our lives, and our goal is to expose it for what it is so we can begin to gain some control over it.

For me, this isn't just about headlines or unknown celebrities. If it were, I probably wouldn't bother to write. For me, it's personal.

AN APOLOGY WILL GET YOU EVERYWHERE

"Never ruin an apology with an excuse." — Benjamin Franklin

When I became an instant parent of four children, I made myself only one promise: I would apologize when I was wrong. That was it. I didn't even promise that I would try my hardest, or would love my newly adopted children "unconditionally," or that I would attend every sporting event and school function. I didn't promise that I wasn't going to get mad or I was going to read to them every night. The only thing I promised myself is that when I was wrong, when I made a mistake, I would apologize.

I figured if there were any one thing I could give my kids that had any lasting value, it would first be the ability to recognize that making mistakes is human and, second, to say "I'm sorry." Somehow, right or wrong, saying

> *Mistakes are what make us human, and apologies are what help us survive our humanity.*

"I'm sorry" even trumped being able to say "I love you." Mistakes are what make us human, and apologies are what help us survive our humanity.

It eventually became a joke between the kids. Whenever one of them got in trouble, another one would try to convince the punished child to just apologize. For whatever reason, even if they were faking, it always made me back off on the punishment when I got an apology. The kids knew that and used it to their "advantage." However, that lesson would be one of the only lessons that would later save our family as shame tore it apart.

Specifically, I remember getting into a raging shouting match with the oldest—our son Troy. As you probably already picked up from the introduction of this book, I had (and still have) a hair trigger, and this particular argument probably involved me either throwing or hitting something as well. Probably, much like his younger sister goaded me into punching a wall, he had triggered my internal shame such that I had to react in anger and rage. I am still not sure why this is my go-to defense when I'm confronted with my shame, but it is.

I don't remember how old he was at the time; he was in seventh grade when we adopted them, so I'm guessing he was in middle school. After going off on him for who knows what, we were walking across the field separating our place from the neighbor's, and it dawned on me that I most likely embedded in him some new-found shame of his own. Like his sister, in my rage, I had probably attempted to communicate to him that he was the stupid one, that *he* was the wrong one. I had most probably attempted to transfer the shame I was feeling about myself onto him. Shame requires us to do that—to unload our perceived badness onto other people.

I stopped him at the fence that separated our properties, realizing I had to attempt to set things straight. I realized I had to at least attempt to confront and acknowledge my own demons in hopes that he would not one day need to transfer that shame onto his own kids, forever perpetuating the saga.

We stopped at the fence and, after I pulled myself together, I told him I was aware young boys learn how to behave from their parents or caretakers, frequently their fathers. Specifically, I said I believed there was the potential for him to see how I just responded to him and think that my behavior was OK. I said, "I hope when you look back at this day, you don't think the way I just spoke to you was OK. It wasn't. I was wrong, and I'm sorry, and I hope you are able to not carry this moment into how you treat your own kids."

Shame will want to prevent us from apologizing. If we are going to apologize, we will have to acknowledge, publically, that we made a mistake. We will have to acknowledge that we have limitations and weaknesses and that whatever action for which we are apologizing is an example of those limitations coming out to hurt another person. Shame wants nothing to do with people becoming publically aware of their limitations.

Shame will then insist that we not back down and admit when we're wrong. Shame requires us to defend ourselves and blame each other. Shame insists we continue to hate, hold grudges, and live resentful, unforgiving lives. Shame's insistence will prevent any form of healthy reconciliation in relationships around the idea that we are all human, flawed, and limited.

LIMITLESS LIMITATIONS

I would not be just a nuffin' my head all full of stuffin' My heart all full of pain. I would dance and be merry, life would be a ding-a-derry, If I only had a brain. —Scarecrow, Wizard of Oz

As Dorothy, the Scarecrow, the Tin Man, and the Cowardly Lion all marched off toward Oz, they reminisced about what would make them complete. Their fears and concerns regarding what was missing in their lives was real—as real as my daughter's need for thin lips and straighter hair. This dilemma speaks to a common malady among anyone introspective enough to think about it: we are all short a few things that might make us "enough."

When our friends traveling the yellow brick road finally get to Oz, all they "need" is for the man behind the curtain to give them some trinket that will offset the way in which they are inherently

The irony is that being human is defined by being limited; if we were without limitations, we would not be human. Being "incomplete" is part of what defines us as human at all.

deficient. The Scarecrow gets a piece of paper, the Lion a goofy little crown that likely came off a stuffed animal, and the Tin Man a hunk of plastic hanging on a pendant. They are now "complete." If it were only so easy.

The irony is that being human is defined by being limited; if we were without limitations, we would not be human. Being "incomplete" is part of what defines us as human at all. What we are truly grieving is the fact that we are human—we have limitations—and our hope is that we can find that trinket to hang around our neck that will convince us we are superhuman. As I discuss later, it was what was driving Eve to be "like God" in the Garden of Eden when she was convinced she should eat the forbidden apple. As I mentioned in the Preface, it's also why it's so difficult to ask for help. When we admit we need help, we admit we are limited and, subsequently, human.

The trinket my daughter Tilonda needed to be complete was a boyfriend. Perhaps many girls do. As a little girl, I don't think she figured she would ever attract a boy. She thought her kinky hair and wide nose would see to that. However, having a boyfriend would also satiate some wound inside her—some need for approval from a boy who maybe, just maybe, thought she was attractive—that maybe she didn't have this overwhelming limitation of her physical traits.

Shame, our fear of being exposed to the world, infects us early in life, and it deeply motivates and manipulates our lives as we age usually in very unhelpful ways. In fact, it is my argument in this book that *shame is the root of all evil.*

CHAPTER 2

Shame: ~~The Good,~~ the Bad, and the Ugly

You cannot shame or belittle people into changing their behaviors (Brown 2008, 1).

"Shame on you" is a rather well-known phrase that's been used over the centuries to get people to behave the way we want them to behave. Therefore, some who have heard my proposition that shame is actually a motivator behind our *poor* decisions have found that to be a challenging idea.

I was doing a radio show for a conservative radio station recently. When doing a show like this, I will inevitably be challenged with the notion that shame is actually a good thing. It seems as though some people in our culture find shame to be a helpful presence that may keep "social ills" in check. For the most part, it seems "social ills" has to do as much with conforming to whatever that group sees as social "norms" as it does with any actual "ills."

The suggestion of this host to me was that we don't have enough shame in our world today, so certain social ills are running rampant. He used unwed pregnancy as his example of how an absence of shame has led us into increased levels of social illness. He suggested, in general, our culture was taking a substantial moral turn toward the ugly and suggested that what we needed was for people to feel a bit more shame—to prevent them from doing "bad things" (again, as defined by his sense of "bad"). He specifically asked me what I thought of girls getting pregnant (ironically, he never mentioned the boys who got the girls pregnant) and wondered if we had a little more shame in the world if people would behave better, not get pregnant, and be less likely to become "moral deviants" and the like.

Brown, who has extensively studied shame, has expressly based her entire life's work on a belief that shame will not change behavioral patterns long term (see Chapter 1 of *I Thought It Was Just Me* [2008]). I don't have in mind to convince anyone of this fact from an academic standpoint—Brown is well versed in and capable of that task, and I suggest you consider some of her work for that argument.

I am a theologian—a studier of God. And what I have found biblically is the foundational evidence for *why* this idea that shame might be a *good* thing is such an unproductive idea. In particular, I find the link between religious people and people who want to *use* shame itself to correct behavior fascinating, given what's actually recorded in the Bible.

One of the most powerful lines from a book in the Bible *that is at the foundation of three major world religions* suggests a world *without* shame was actually God's intent. Ironically, "in the beginning" there was no shame . . .

Genesis 2 [25]Adam and his wife were both naked, and they felt no shame.

If, after everything God created that was necessary for humanity to function was soundly placed into our lives and shame was not among them, I think it's safe to assume it's not a helpful force (at least from a biblical perspective).

Ironically, this verse is also the opening line from the seminal book on shame: *Healing the Shame that Binds You* (Bradshaw 1998). It's not a religious book but a book on bondage and freedom that uses this line, my favorite line, as its grand opener. It's a book on the story of humanity through the eyes of a man—the book's author, a wildly successful human being in whatever way you hope to gauge such things—suffering the debilitating effects of shame. It's a book that is as much the story of human history and human life in general as it is a book about your life, and my life, and his life in particular.

> *The fact that he already wrote his story should only embolden me to write my own.*

When I first read that book, I was in shock and felt—wait for it—ashamed. I felt ashamed because someone had beaten me to this scholarly piece. This author felt the exact same way I did and *beat me* to the book that sold 1.3 million copies and was a *New York Times* best seller! He even used my opening passage from the Bible! What on earth, I wondered, is the point of writing my book now!!?!

Then emerges a different voice—battling to be heard. I hear a voice that is screaming that 1.3 million people experienced something positive in his work. I hear a voice reminding me that 1.3 million people resonated with this message. I began to hear a voice that said, "You may *not* be crazy." It's pretty unusual for me to hear a positive voice, so I let it stew for a while—and I kept writing.

The reason I kept writing, as you may already know by now, is because it's more important to tell your story than to provide any "new information" about shame. The more we are able to see that we are not alone in our battle with this situation, the braver we will all become in dealing with it. The fact that he already wrote his story should only embolden me to write my own. My shame tells me that it's about the information and that smarter people are out there who have already spoken to this topic. Shame would prefer I cower silently in a corner and keep to myself. No immediate pain will come from that and shame itself can remain hidden.

Clearly, expert after expert acknowledges that shame is a universal condition among all people groups regardless of race, gender, ethnicity, or age. In fact, I had so many quotes in this book from each of the other books I read, I eventually had to eliminate the majority of them. So, when I proclaim that shame is universal in this way, it really isn't earth-shattering news for anyone that's read a book on shame. However, I would like to better understand how such a universal event came about anyway. How could we all be suffering from the exact same condition, and what exactly *is* this condition?

> *Vulnerability was never bad. It was how we were created. How we feel about and react to our vulnerability is what's gotten us into trouble.*

As a result, I've come to believe that all of humanity has been infected with a rather toxic and frequently fatal *virus*, for lack of a better word, that's often referred to as "shame." The fact that John Bradshaw's work sold 1.3 million copies—as well as the work of modern vulnerability evangelist Brené Brown being so popular—is because the condition and its effects are so rampant and common. Although the virus itself seems to affect everyone differently and to different degrees, it seems to be always there in every heart.

The difficulty is that it's so contagious and rather elusive. We tend to pick it up like chickenpox at the earliest age—first from our parents or others in our immediate family who are definitely vessels of the contagion themselves (since we all have it). But then it seems to grow and aggravate as we go through our early years where, by our teens, the symptoms are nearly universal in scope if not in kind.

It's also difficult to treat because we typically find ourselves treating the symptoms and not the virus. In the same way, we might keep popping antacid to deal with a gut ache, but we never put any energy into finding out why our gut is actually aching to begin with. Is it stress? The flu? Anxiety? Until we deal with the root cause of our surface issues (like anger for me), we simply keep treating the symptoms, and the virus lives on to fight another day.

It's here I find the story in Genesis so captivating. I'm not laying claim to the truth of the story itself, and arguing whether or not the events are literal is of no use to me. In fact, it seems to perhaps even hold more truth as a great allegory to how humanity ended up the way it did than as a description validating the existence of a God who created all things.

It fascinatingly demonstrates how, since as far back as recorded history exists, we've been attempting to explain this illness called *shame*, where it came from and its effects on our lives. It should also not be lost on us that this issue is dealt with at the very initiation of at least the three major world religions that find their home in this book.

Genesis begins, as many know, spending two chapters scrolling through the acts of creation. You see the earth and sky, then plants and animals, and finally culminating in humanity and our role in life to "tend creation." It's idyllic. It concludes with something of this watershed statement that creates a pause in human history where, just for a split second, things were as they were intended to be. It also seems to serve as an ominous foreboding of where things are soon to be headed . . .

Genesis 2 [25]Adam and his wife were both naked, and they felt no shame.

It's from the last line in Genesis 2—this pause before humanity heads into the infamous fall—that I take my definition of the word *shame*. Shame is whatever it is we experience when we are naked, exposed, defenseless, standing bare to the world for its detailed examination of our unhidden reality—everything that makes us "us," so to speak. Shame is what we experience when we are completely vulnerable. Vulnerability was never bad. It was how we were created. How we feel about and react to our vulnerability is what's gotten us into trouble.

In this moment, at the end of Genesis 2, man and woman could be seen "in all their glory" and felt no shame. How rare that might be for any of us—from any race, religion, age, or culture on this planet—to be seen in our entirety, every nook and cranny, every thought, word, and deed, and not feel shame. Every failure exposed and every weakness highlighted. This condition of facing our vulnerability without fear (shame) no longer exists—*if* it ever really did—according to this ancient translation of events.

From the perspective of any faith path that uses the book of Genesis as its starting point, you can quickly see that God created everything good and, specifically, *there was no shame*. If God didn't need it to keep things in line, then neither should we.

The final thing I want to emphasize about this idea is that the "bad" behavior we are hoping to prevent with more shame generally stems from a hope that people will be more like us—that they will conform to whatever standard we are holding. This too finds its root in shame. The more people that are "like us" and hold our values, the less exposed we feel so we try to get people to conform to our standards. This also allows us to project an image that our norms are "right" and theirs are "wrong," which is also required by shame.

Going forward, you will notice my use of biblical examples. I don't intend to use Bible verses as a means to prove any specific religion more valid than another. I use the Bible as a means of accomplishing a few things:

1. **Demonstrate how long humanity has been battling this condition.**
2. **Demonstrate that we are no better or any worse than any other time throughout history—dating as far back as the Bible, anyway.**
3. **Dispell the argument that shame is a good thing.**

If you are of a religious persuasion that believes the account in Genesis is supposed to speak to life today and still suggest shame is a good thing, I hope to demonstrate that argument has no basis in Scripture. In fact, shame not only does not promote "good behavior" but led to the first and subsequent acts of human "sin."

A RED HERRING TO THE RESCUE: SIN VS. SHAME

"The fall" has always been a story about sin—at least in Christianity. It's been a story about that first act of "bad" perpetrated by humanity. Little if any attention is paid to the more insidious condition that generated the first rebellious act or, I argue, every single one since.

The typical Christian viewpoint tells us it was always the devil's intent to sidetrack us with a "symptom" of our condition so we never look to the disease itself. And although many of us believe ourselves to be freed from sin through Christ, we are also quick to acknowledge that the desire to do so never fades. The desire to pursue our own self-interest over the interest of others never completely trails off. It can, in fact, get worse. Part of that is because we keep dealing with the symptom (sin) instead of the disease (shame).

I recently had lunch with a friend who had a typical experience of feeling completely free of sin and shame when he became a Christian. I never had that experience so it fascinates me when others have. So, I grilled him some more on the experience and asked him why, later, the experience of being dirty and worthless would come back again. I wondered what really happened in the "washing" experience.

He described the way shame had its tentacles in him—much like my son would describe it. He said that, like a weed, you could chop it down, but that it would find a way to sprout anew into your life when you least expected it.

As quick as we are to get sidetracked with symptoms and a drive to see quick results, we spend our time there—focusing on sin—and spend very little time looking at the actual disease. We chop down the weed but never deal with the root. This is the great red herring of Christianity.

A red herring tactic is used for various purposes whenever someone wants to throw someone off the *real* trail of what they are attempting to obtain.

The proposition from the snake to the woman in the garden has always been described as an issue of pride—something evil lurking in the woman, her desire to "be like God." Readings of this story by Christian audiences tend to portray the woman as a villain, dark in soul, instead of as a fellow traveler deserving our empathy. We never ask the really important questions: Why did she want to be like God to begin with? Was it pride or hubris, or was it something deeper? Is this story about sin and "doing bad," or is there a greater issue at stake? I was about to get my answer to that question . . .

*　*　*

Dinner was over, and I was having a couple drinks with some salespeople afterward. We had spent the day listening to remarks from our CEO at a district sales meeting on the East Coast, and it was time to kick back at the bar.

How we got on the subject of shame is a story for later. However, as I was describing to them this book I was writing (and needing to capture the story we just heard for the book), I found myself careening through Genesis with these two folks who had little church background. Looking back, this seems like an odd place to find yourself—drinking beer with coworkers talking about Genesis. My own inner critic can't help even now wonder how odd that must have felt for them or how weird they may have found that experience.

Anyway, I got to the part about what the snake said to the woman— "You will be like God"—and I stopped and asked them both, "What was the snake actually saying?" And the female sales-person I was with (Ally), without hesitation and without prodding said, "You are not enough"—as if she'd heard that voice over and over again in her own soul

> *We chop down the weed but never deal with the root. This is the great red herring of Christianity.*

for years. "That's what the snake was saying. You are not enough!" It wasn't so much the words she used as *how* she used them. She added the exclamation point as if discovering something—maybe about the Bible, maybe about herself.

This is my definition of the complicated concept of shame from here on out: fear of being exposed to others for who you are, limited and "not enough."

> *Contained in the experience of shame is the piercing awareness of ourselves as fundamentally deficient in some vital way as a human being. To live with shame is to experience the very essence or heart of the self as wanting* (Kaufman 1992, 9).

This voice is most dangerous when it's embedded in our sub-conscious, which is why it probably prefers to operate there. Then, we can act out and be manipulated by it without ever being able to resolve the issue. When it becomes conscious, as I describe later, we finally have an opportunity to object. It's why Ally reacted in a way to suggest she found something new that she always knew was there.

"The root of shame," says Kaufman, "lies in sudden unexpected exposure." This is what happened to Eve in the garden. She was sud-denly exposed as "not enough"—something we humans experience on a daily basis. So now, where this garden was once a place where humanity was naked and felt no shame, there was suddenly full frontal awareness of being exposed.

When I pose the same question to people who have a history with the church, they don't see the same events. They tend to look at Eve not with empathy but contempt because the snake was not playing on her inner fears but her desire for power.

Ally, on the other hand, views Eve with empathy. Ally has been there. Ally doesn't see a woman obsessed with power, she sees a woman suddenly aware of her smallness and vulnerability. Why would Eve even desire such power unless she had some inner fear of being powerless or vulnerable or not being enough?

Most interesting to me is that the voice Ally heard so quickly is the same voice in my daughter's head and, if Ally is right, a voice first heard and recorded millennia ago by the first woman (if you at least follow the allegoric value of the story). Interestingly, my daughter is a dark-skinned African American woman whose family of origin was very broken. Ally, on the other hand, is light-skinned blonde who was raised by two parents and very much professionally employed. The same voice resides in each of them, and it was first uttered at the very onset of human creation. You are not enough . . .

So, when the woman is told that eating the fruit will make her like God—it will give her something she does not possess. The snake introduces the woman to shame, which is an awareness of her shortcomings and limitations. The snake doesn't have the woman's attention because the woman has a lofty view of herself (pride); instead, the snake has her attention because she is suddenly afraid of her limitations and, *worse, someone else is aware of them, too.*

As Kaufman says, "Defeats, failures, or rejections need no longer be actual, but only perceived as such. Simple awareness of a limitation may be sufficient to count as a mortal wounding of the self, a new confirmation of inherent defectiveness" (Kaufman 1992, 115).

The snake introduces the woman to the possibility that there's something wrong with her and the way she is made. It is the first time in recorded history that a woman is offered a look at herself in a mirror and comes to believe she's less than she is supposed to be.

After that, it's not a far leap from that fear in your mind about how you are "less than you should be" to making all attempts possible to resolve that issue. Eve is no different than my daughter or any manner of women (or men) anywhere facing the angry voice inside telling you that you are not enough and to do whatever it takes to make yourself "enough."

This is where the wheels start coming off the wagon.

We have all been chasing the red herring of sin (or our "actions" to use a non-biblical word) as the root issue instead of getting at what causes the undesirable action to begin with. Similarly, we chase bad behaviors all around the block. We attempt to treat things like low self-esteem, depression, violence, and narcissism as if they have separate beginnings when, in reality, they are just different symptoms of the same disease: shame and our fear that our "not enoughness" is going to go public.

Ironically, the words the snake put into Eve's ear, that she was not enough, weren't a lie. She is not. Neither is Ally. Neither are my kids, and neither am I. We are all human, which means we are all foundationally limited beings in one way or another. *The snake was telling the truth—that's the horrible irony in the story.* We've come to know the snake as a liar. The lie is that being "not enough" is a bad thing and is something we need to fix. The snake never has to utter the lie because our subconscious will do that work all by itself.

Until we begin to get at the source, the disease itself, that tells us this lie that being limited is a bad thing, all we can do is put cold compresses on the symptoms of rage, depression, fear, indecision (the list goes on forever, it seems). Like aspirin to a headache, we can take some meds for the depression, we can go to anger management classes and learn to take deep breaths before we speak, and read all the self-help books on decision making—all of which may provide some relief, and relief is *not* a bad thing! I've had to employ many of them myself. But our goal is to get at the root issue—the root of all this evil.

SHAME, SIN, GUILT. REPEAT AS NEEDED.

I often get challenged with the concept of which came first, sin or shame, especially because I spend so much of my time in religious circles. Come to think of it, I'm not sure people outside religious circles care. They just want to get a handle on their poor decisions! The pragmatic part of me wants to throw up my hands on this issue and call it a draw. However, I think this is a case where words or semantics matter in moving toward a resolution.

I was preaching a message on Genesis to a congregation near my hometown. It was a well-established congregation of exceptionally well-versed congregants. When I asked the couple of salespeople why Adam was hiding, and they didn't know, they had an excuse—they were not versed in the Bible nor were they church-goers of any particular stripe. But this congregation represented a group of people for whom church and Bible education had been part of their lives for generations.

I asked them if they knew why Adam was hiding. With a resounding voice, they replied, "Because he was afraid!"

"Correct!" I said. "Why was he afraid?"

Silence.

Then, a brave voice in the back said, "Because he sinned."

While this is the standard response I get from a church, I could tell from the general silence in the room that there was much more uncertainty about why exactly he was afraid. And, as you'll recall, **understanding exactly why we are doing what we are doing is the path we have to take to really begin to find the core issues in our lives.**

I'm curious where we got the impression that Adam was afraid because he had sinned. Perhaps we have this image from our own childhood of hiding from our parents for fear of being punished for something we had done. We look at Adam afraid, and we naturally place ourselves there as children after doing something our parents instructed us not to do.

The problem? That's not why Adam says he's afraid. He did not say he was afraid because he had sinned or because he did something bad. The reason Adam gave for hiding from God was that *he was afraid.*

Of course, following our pattern, we must ask *why* he was afraid. At this point, you could *still* say he was afraid because he'd sinned, not unlike you did as a child after filling the squirt gun with toilet water and spraying your sister's hair with it. The problem? That's not why he says he was afraid.

Adam didn't say he was afraid because he'd done something bad, he said he was afraid because *he was naked.* He was afraid because he would be seen in all his glory. He was afraid, not because he *had done* something bad, but because it would now be obvious that *he was* something bad. Humanity was naked, and they felt shame (fear), and it's *this* issue that undergirds our disintegration as humans.

This, then, is what gives birth to the two primary outcomes of shame:

1. **Separation (hiding) from each other and God and**
2. **Making bad decisions to make ourselves something we will never be: enough.**

The terms of sin and guilt must also be understood in context of shame. Things get a bit tricky here, because we have to agree that sin and guilt are predominantly religious experiences. If there is no God, there is no sin. However, the majority of humanity has a sense that sin exists insomuch as it means "doing something wrong" or "not doing what is right."

Regardless what you think about sin or wrongdoing, we certainly know guilt exists. Guilt is frequently described as the feeling we get when we sin or when we do something bad, and is an emotion with

which we quickly become acquainted with from our earliest days—
as early as we begin to understand what is good and what is bad.

As we previously discussed, while sin is typically thought of as
"doing something bad," guilt is the feeling associated with having
done that bad thing. *Shame is not a sense of having done something
bad but of being something bad.* It's the difference I hear in my voice
when I scold myself for *doing* something stupid, and the name I have
for myself for *being* stupid. The latter is, as they say, ontological—it
has to do with the core of my being.

> ### Shame is not a sense of having done something bad but of being something bad.

The serpent used shame
by reminding the woman she
was "not enough" to entice her
to "sin" in an attempt to gain
"enoughness." Once we become
aware of our lack of "enoughness"
and specifically we become aware
that someone else is aware of the situation, we must fix or hide that
situation. The fall into sin, however we define that, is easy because we
must either try to fix our inadequacy or hide it. Thus, it is shame that
is the source—the sin is the symptom. As Curt Thompson has said,
"It [shame] is *the* emotional feature out of which all that we call sin
emerges" (2015, 99 [emphasis his]).

Still, sin/guilt and shame exist in a very symbiotic relationship—
feeding off each other. We are evidence-based creatures, and the
evidence actually suggests that we are not God, as the snake suggested—that we are not enough. As I mentioned previously, no one
ever said the snake lied in his suggestion to Eve that she was not
enough. Eve just didn't like the suggestion!! The more bad stuff we
do, the more we become aware (consciously or subconsciously) of
the possibility that we are fundamentally a bad person.

The evidence actually points to the fact that we *do* have shortcomings, limitations, and imperfections. This adds to our shame and
self-contempt, which causes us to either fix, hide, or blame all the

more furiously. There is no end to this hamster's wheel and begets an exercise in futility. That, my own life has taught me, is death even though I am still breathing.

This is the danger of confronting actual wrong deeds of individuals—whether in ourselves, our children, people we love, coworkers, etc. We run the very real risk of solidifying the notion that person has about their self-worth, which might just cause them to do bad all the more. Or we simply make people defensive, causing them to deny there was ever any bad done.

This is where self-contempt can become most pronounced—when we're "busted."

THE VENOM IS SELF-CONTEMPT

One bright, sunny fall afternoon, I was trying to corral a calf with navel ill so she could get her antibiotics. As I made my way through the pasture, I tripped on my shoes that I always refused to tie and heard that scolding refrain in my head to myself: "you #$#@% stupid @#$& idiot." It's a pet name I have for myself that I use with shocking regularity. I'm fairly certain I know the origin of those particular words and will spare you the details, but suffice it to say, as with most things, they were established in me quite early.

If you knew me personally, I'm certain that revelation might take you as quite a surprise. I'm fairly well accomplished in my profession, my wife and I successfully raised a sibling group of four children, I started a cattle farm with no history or training in agriculture, and started a ground-up, new church with no experience in ministry.

I have advanced degrees in ministry and a rather fancy title: The Reverend Doctor Rick Patterson. Yet the title I use in my own head for me is, "you #$#@% stupid @#$& idiot" (my editor insisted I not use the actual language, as she feared it was too offensive for most readers to stomach).

But, on this day, this bright, sunny fall afternoon in a calving pasture in southwest Michigan, it would end differently. The refrain rang through my head the way it had 18 million times before: "you #$#@% stupid @#$& idiot." How could you be so &*^#@ stupid??!" But, for some reason, in this particular moment, I actually stopped to ask myself, "Who talks to people that way?" Has my own head become the *Jerry Springer Show*? I won't allow this show on my TV but, for some reason, I allow it to play through my own head aimed directly at myself! I am incapable of allowing myself the opportunity to make mistakes or be wrong. That's shame. This is a concept that has been long understood by experts in the field of shame and a cycle I seemed to be living on an almost daily basis.

> *Mistakes, which ought to be expected in the course of daily functioning, become occasions of agonizing self-torture . . . [as a result] the self may inflict unrelenting suffering upon the self. And that internal shame spiral is unleashed which can all but consume the self* (Kaufman 1992, 115).

I was on a plane weeks later, trapped in an Arkansas-bound steel tube with only my thoughts and a couple books dealing with self-contempt. The heavens seemed to suddenly open to reveal the truth about the levels of contempt I felt for myself. It seemed I had been developing a growing awareness of the sea of self-contempt I had in my soul, but I never appreciated the *depth* of the sea until that moment.

Let me just pause here to define *contempt*. While I often use the word *hatred* to equate to contempt (self-hatred), a more accurate way of looking at the word *contempt* is "despised" or "looked down upon as worthless or beneath consideration." *Contempt* is very much a feeling in your gut—a disgust for a thing because it is so far beneath that which it is being compared. When we have self-contempt, we are comparing ourselves to some standard by which we are not measuring up.

The contempt or disgust I had for myself is a great example

because it had no basis in fact. I was looking down at something (myself) as having very limited value when, in reality, it was of great value. However, to the point of this book, this contempt, this way we view ourselves, was dictating many of my decisions. We make decisions, one after another, seeking some sort of redemption for the person we believe we have become—a person in need of constant rebuke and punishment—even though our

> *Guilt says you did something bad, shame says you are something bad.*

lives have been quite successful. Sadly, we may not even be aware of how we view ourselves until we have a "moment in the pasture" like I experienced.

Again, this is the difference between guilt and shame. Guilt says you *did* something bad, shame says you *are* something bad. And, this level of self-contempt, this hatred for who you are, frequently unrealized in all of us, is what is driving our path to destruction. In my case, the hatred was so bad that even when I became aware of the verbal abuse I was leveling against myself, I refused to come to my own defense. I refused to do for myself what I would do for any other human being.

TIME FOR A THROW DOWN

When my girls were in high school, their school's boys' basketball team had made it to the state quarter finals. While at the game, my daughter Tilonda was mouthing off with some of her friends and tossing spit wads in various directions at various folks. This behavior itself did not take me by surprise, but little did I know where it was heading.

Tilonda and her friends were confronted by some parents in the crowd, so I went and extracted my daughter from the fracas before it got out of hand. Things seemed to settle down until the game was over. I had lost track of my daughter only to see her, mouth wide open, saying who knows what to this same family. I again went to extract my daughter but, as I moved in her direction, I took a split second to look back over my shoulder to see the adult gentleman she was addressing. I then saw him mouth these words, "Shut your black ass."

I'm not sure what triggered me exactly. Was his size compared to my daughter, or perhaps his age? Most likely, I think it was that he singled out the one attribute about her "self" she most disliked—her blackness. He singled out the one and only way he could describe my daughter as subhuman in his estimation. He was calling my daughter ugly.

In that moment, whatever my daughter had been doing (out of her own shame) was suddenly irrelevant to me. I did a 180 to head in the direction of the gentleman who had addressed my daughter. He was probably 5 to 10 years older than me and certainly 5 to 6 inches taller and 50 pounds heavier. My fists were clenched and I had one consideration in mind: this man was going to be dismantled today. I'm not sure if I was angry at him as much as I hurt for my daughter—already tortured by society for her race and appearance. I was probably mostly angry *at* him, truth be known.

Things moved in slow motion from there. I saw the face of the high school principal looking into my eyes—he knew what was happening and where I was going but seemed powerless to stop it. He knew this was not going to end well for anyone.

I looked back at the gentleman and thought how odd it was—given his size—that he should have such fear in his eyes—or maybe it was shame. Maybe in that moment he felt self-contempt for allowing those words to come out of his mouth. I don't know. I didn't care.

I gave no thought whatsoever to the fact that I was a pastor in town or how my action might not be a good example of patience and calm to my daughter. I never once wondered what Jesus would do nor did I consider that this was a decision I might deeply regret one day. I had no empathy for him and his own situation that would require him to lash out at a teenage girl in that manner. I had one intention only, and that intention was to dehumanize him and treat him like the animal I perceived him to be—like the animal he thought my daughter was.

I drew within a couple of yards, and his eyes turned awkwardly down. It was the face of shame.

I didn't care.

As I took my last step in his direction, I was physically stopped by a fellow quite a bit shorter than me who was pushing into my chest as if he were trying to push a sack of cement back up on a shelf somewhere. He was moving me off my feet and back onto my heels, pushing me back, repeating the words, "He's not worth it," over and over and over as he moved me outside the stadium foyer and into the street.

At this point, I had no idea what was happening and soon found myself—at his physical insistence—outside the foyer of the gym under the lights with him still in my face chanting, "He's not worth it."

It's those words I wonder about today. "He's not worth it." Certainly, he must have that perception of himself to denigrate a child half his size in the way she was most vulnerable. Perhaps it was not much different than the *Playboy* Playmate snapping a photo of the overweight woman, at the gym, doing her best to push through the material shame she could not hide. I wonder if he knew his worth, would this guy have had to attack my daughter at

> *By identifying and ostracizing the deficiencies of others, we never have to deal with the fact that it is actually we who are weak and vulnerable.*

the place where she was most vulnerable or could he have simply walked away?

Perhaps my daughter had somehow struck him where he was most vulnerable as well—the same way my younger daughter Tapricia had struck me when she rolled her eyes professing my stupidity. That's what we humans do, isn't it? Attack where people are most vulnerable and when *we* feel most vulnerable and exposed?

To an extent, I consider Eve had been bitten by the snake that day in the garden. The venom the snake produced, the material causing damage, was self-hatred. Carl Jung believed this idea, self-hatred, to be the "essence of the whole moral problem."

We have a self-help mantra today in which *we try to convince ourselves that we are enough. We* need *to be enough.* All the self-help books attempt to help us understand that even though the basic principle of humanity says we are flawed, imperfect, that we *can* be perfect. That's a lie. The reality is, we are human, and that means we are flawed and very much *not* enough. Being human also means we are fundamentally vulnerable beings. We can be hurt. Coming to grips with these realities of what it means to be human is of greatest importance if we are to become resilient to shame. Perhaps it means we actually need each other. The lie is that we need to be "enough" or that being "enough" is somehow even achievable. This is what makes us grab for the apple even after being told it's not good for us.

The sad part of this is that not only does this fear of not being enough demoralize us *personally*, it has lasting repercussions on how we treat others. Instead of coming to grips with the fact we are all flawed, that none of us are actually God, we frequently, in our fear and shame, chase out, ostracize, mock, or belittle anything that may be less "enough" than we are. By identifying and ostracizing the deficiencies of others, we never have to deal with the fact that it is actually we who are weak and vulnerable.

CHAPTER 3

Survival of the ~~Fittest~~ Flawed

"He was a killer, a thing that preyed, living on the things that lived, unaided, alone, by virtue of his own strength and prowess, surviving triumphantly in a hostile environment where only the strong survive." —Jack London, *The Call of the Wild*

The destructive power of the natural world has never ceased to amaze me. From the youngest age, I have been enthralled with animal shows; Marlin Perkins and *Mutual of Omaha's Wild Kingdom* was a never-miss show growing up. As I aged and animal cinematography became more advanced, they were better able to capture the brutality of the natural world—to the point I can no longer watch it. I remember a bumper sticker on the car in front of me some years ago: *Nature Is My God.* I remember thinking to myself, "Your God is a mean-spirited, unforgiving, and sadistic tyrant."

The fate of the injured or downtrodden was always bleak. On all the animal shows I watched, when an animal was injured, it would likely meet a quick demise at the hands of some predator or, perhaps, its own herdmates. It was suggested that at least their death came quickly and so was somehow "good." "Not good" was the slow, lingering death—or death by evisceration as the wild dogs and hyenas of Africa practice.

I specifically remember an *Animal Planet* episode catching the scene when an albino gazelle was desperately just trying to be one of the herd, but it was tormented relentlessly by the rest of the herd in an attempt to drive it out. The narrator wondered if it was a survival mechanism because the albino animal was so easy to spot by predators. Obviously, I had no basis for knowing this, but I envisioned the sorrow of the albino gazelle that just wanted to be one of the herd and, because there were no mirrors, probably had no way of knowing why it was being so harshly treated.

I wish I could say this was simply a survival mechanism relegated to the "animal" kingdom. It's not. It's part and parcel of our human experience as well. For some reason, an entire culture had convinced my daughter that she was ugly—a stigma that still carries into her adult years. That's the power of cultural destruction and our individual need to make someone "the ugly one" at all.

There is something inside us that *needs* to do this as well—for fear of our own animalistic survival. Only it's typically not our physical survival we fear for when we ostracize someone from our human "herd," it is *emotional survival.* There is something inside our humanity, fearing we individually are not enough, that causes us to focus on and force out anyone who is obviously *more* "not enough" than we are, all as part of the manipulation of shame. If the rest of the world is focused on the "not enoughness" of someone else, they won't have time to see our own deficiencies and we will live to emotionally survive another day.

Moore warned us that *"to the extent that you refuse to acknowledge*

the enemy within you, then emotionally you must project it somewhere
else . . . you have to expel your badness onto someone else" (Moore 2003,
19/20). It's a survival mechanism.

STICKS AND STONES . . .

While my eldest daughter Tilonda struggled with her race, my
middle daughter TiShanté faced another challenge that was no less
demoralizing. She grew up with a bed-wetting problem—again,
for reasons that would likely be self-evident to anyone who knew
her history.

As a result, by the time she started school, she was given the nick-
name "Pissy Coon Balloon" by the adults in her life to highlight
her deficiencies and shortcomings. I don't have all the background
on this story. Perhaps they mistakenly thought shaming her would
get her to change her behavior. Perhaps they were just struggling
with their own shame, so they needed to project their ugliness on
someone smaller. I don't know. What I know is how it affected her
own self-understanding.

Whenever she would get in trouble at our house or couldn't
understand something, she would sit on her bed and bang the back
of her head against the wall chanting, "I hate myself, I hate myself,
I hate myself," and throw in the occasional, "I just want to die,"
for good measure. I had never seen such explicit self-contempt in
another human being in my life. In these moments, she defined for
me what "self-contempt" looked like. She literally found herself to be
of no worth whatsoever. My wife and I needed to repeatedly come to
her aid against the voices in her head in her early years, and it even
ended up with several trips to the hospital.

I again find myself in shock that one adult human can talk to
a child in this manner. And, more to the point of this book, I am
compelled to understand what it is inside an adult that takes us to
our basest animalistic selves such that we act no better than gazelle.

What possible value does an adult human being derive out of being this way to a child? Be assured, however, we do find value in it—I know this firsthand.

Lest I look like a hero in all this, I must recognize that I too spent time as a bully in school, demoralizing other children who could not defend themselves. I too beat my fair share of "albino gazelles" into submission to make sure they understood they were "less than" the normal gazelle in the herd.

The one I remember most distinctly was Charles; he was routinely abused by other kids in the neighborhood and on the playground. Since Charles was one of the few kids who was smaller and weaker than me, he received my abuse. Ironically, he was also the only boy in my neighborhood to hang out with, so he was also my most frequent companion.

On this particular day in middle school, I was harassing Charles on the playground. I kept pushing him down every time he'd try to get up—for probably half an hour. The warning bell went off that it was time to come back inside, and I just kept pushing Charles down. As the clock ticked, and all the other students had made their way into the building, I made a run for it. I was faster. I beat Charles to the building before the tardy bell went off and pulled the door shut and locked it.

The gratification I received was a momentary soothing of my own weak soul that required some recognition that I was not the weakest one out there. My shame needed that soothing in order to cope with the horrific reality that it was only a matter of time before the herd turned on me if I didn't find a more compelling target. It made me feel momentarily good inside and I didn't know why.

Charles hit the door and, in full grief, he finally lost his will. He began to sob. Me on one side of the door holding the lock, Charles on the other, sobbing. I had effectively boxed out the albino gazelle at Parchment Middle School. In that moment, though, as young as I was, I realized that the enemy was inside my own self. I was horrified at me. Sadly, that sort of self-hatred tends to lead only one place: even more harmful actions.

Many forms of this person-on-person abuse are obvious and direct, as the examples depict. Others, many others, are more hidden and underhanded.

Sadly, for some reason, when we exert our power over someone or something weaker, for a minute, it gives our wounded soul some wicked form of relief. Frequently, that relief is frail and fleeting as we also deeply regret the kind of person we are who is willing and able of doing such a thing, which then generates more self-hatred requiring us to kill again.

> *Sadly, for some reason, when we exert our power over someone or something weaker, for a minute, it gives our wounded soul some wicked form of relief.*

I had a female friend proof-read this book before I published it. It made her reflect on a scenario in which she had been involved. She's a happily single person who had decided to move herself and her dog into the suburbs after a recent promotion at work. She found herself a place she loved and that she and her dog could call home—even though it was mostly populated by young couples with kids.

The first lady my friend met in the yard was immediately curious about whether or not my friend was married. Why this is the first question we ask singles is itself an issue that deserves follow-up. It's also an issue that will frequently produce a shame response in the single person. This person will frequently, to varying degrees by individual, feel a sudden jolt of exposure for being "not enough." This is one reason why there is such a pathological level of poorly chosen life partners in the world—we are hunting for a mate so that we will somehow "become enough" or minimally become what the world insists we should be.

My friend's response was polite; she'd probably heard the question a hundred times before. She said, "Nope, no husband. Just me and my dog."

The neighbor's reaction at that point is what I call "going for the kill." She said, "Well, at least you have him."

Now reading this story, many of you consider two things; the first is how absurd the entire thing is. The second is an awareness of how common it is. The interesting reaction was that of my friend who actually began to wonder if, in fact, there was something "wrong" with her. That's shame language. *Not that she* did *something bad by being single but that it was evidence that she* was *something bad*—that there was something wrong with her.

We must not forget the likely reason the neighbor insisted on being condescending in the first place. The reason she used such language to begin with was likely her own shame, her own need in her soul to fight her own battle that there was likely something "wrong" about her own self. By transferring that "wrongness" onto my friend, it likely gave her a brief respite from her own shame. But it was likely brief, only to come raging back when she realized how "stupid" she was for making such a statement.

Again, catch the shame language. It wasn't that she made a stupid remark, it's that she was stupid for making the remark. And her shame grows. I call this the *poison ivy effect*. We all know if you scratch your poison ivy, it will give immediate and blissful relief. However, we all also know the horrific itching that follows in short order, demanding to be scratched again only all the harder.

This infection—this need to compensate for our own smallness, this need to hurt and

> **It wasn't that she made a stupid remark, it's that she was stupid for making the remark. And her shame grows. I call this the poison ivy effect.**

abuse—is hidden in each of us and is almost instinctual. It's no longer an animalistic need for the survival of the fittest. But it's still an animalistic need for survival: the survival of our weak psyches to know there's someone out there slower than us, fatter than us, dumber than us, weaker than us. When we scratch the itch, it does give momentary relief—as my own example with Charles demonstrated. But the itch comes raging back even worse when we consider what kind of person we must be for behaving the way we did.

There is an exception to the poison ivy effect: The person we most frequently attack is ourselves, and we never seem to feel bad after doing so.

* * *

I remember the first fist fight I saw at school. I wish it had been the only fist fight but there were going to be many of them. I was in sixth grade and was standing outside the art room. They were eighth graders so I didn't know their names. One was white and the other black, I remember that. I remember it because we didn't have many black students in my school.

I guess it wasn't much of a fight. The white kid punched the black kid in the face while the rest of the students circled around and chanted something I don't remember. The black kid fell down, got back up, and walked off.

Most of the fights I saw ended that way. Even the one I was in myself.

What struck me about fist fights was how humiliating the experience must be for the loser. I never thought about the physical pain or even if there was any physical pain. All I could feel—even at that age—was the sharp sting of exposure that must truly come with being found out to be the weaker.

I assume I was able to feel that because I had empathy. I knew that shame somehow and not because it ever happened to me—I committed myself to avoiding it at all costs. I had to avoid being exposed in that manner.

Oddly, the one fight I was in involved Charles—the kid I bullied throughout most of my middle school years. We—me, Charles, and another neighborhood kid—had just gotten off the bus in front of our house. At this point he was bullying Charles. I felt the shame so deeply for Charles (I know how jacked up this story sounds—that's what shame does—it tells jacked up stories). I was able to experience how small he must constantly feel and how ashamed he must constantly feel. The next thing I know, I hit the kid who was hitting Charles.

That was it. Just like the fight outside the art room. One punch and the other kid walked off holding his face, most likely deeply ashamed. Of course, that was only the beginning as I was soon wanted by the friends of the kid I hit. That too is how shame multiplies . . .

Oddly, being empathetic or compassionate toward your own self is a tool that seems completely missing from my toolbox even though I had great empathy for others when they were getting beat up. As *I've already mentioned, I was perfectly willing to come to Charles' aid in my driveway but am consistently unwilling to come to my own aid against myself and I, quite frankly, am my own worst enemy.*

The difference, I think, is deep down we all know Charles didn't deserve what he got. We all know my daughters didn't deserve what they got. *No* victims deserve what they get. Yet, deep down, it seems to me, we think we deserve what we get even when we are victims of our own selves—something my sister was about to teach me.

* * *

My sister, who is a year older, and I got into a fight. How is it possible that I'm still fighting with my sister at what must be at least the midpoint of my life? Have I outgrown nothing?

I'm rather embarrassed (ashamed) of myself to give all the grade school details of our argument, but suffice it to say, I had hurt her feelings. In a rush of thoughtless moves because I felt pressed for time, I forgot something I should have remembered, and it hurt her—as it probably should have. That caused her to attack me (unjustly so I felt), which then required me to defend myself (a shame response).

Let's pause right here and call this the "shame spiral" of our almost daily existence as human beings and the fodder of almost all daytime television. One person attacks (instead of listens) out of hurt. The other person defends themselves (instead of listens) out of pride (aka shame). The attacking person then feels worse, so they dig in deeper, and soon we are off to the shame races.

I can't remember who exactly tapped the brakes on this particular spiral—fun as it was for all involved—but eventually, we somehow got to the heart of the matter. It came out in our discussion that my sister feels a great deal of shame for a wide array of issues. Although she was ashamed of herself, *she was quite convinced I was likely ashamed of her for the same reasons.* This is also something 99% of humans accomplish with ease. We transfer our feelings about ourselves onto others, which makes us believe *they* think about us the way we think about us. Frequently there is nothing further from the truth. However, logic won't stop us from developing a hatred for another person who we think is ashamed of us even though no such feelings actually exist.

For example, because I think I am "the stupid one," I assume others do as well. So, when my daughter rolls her eyes or my wife has a different opinion than I do, I transfer my shame onto them and assume they also think I am the stupid one, which makes me defend myself even though I may never have actually been attacked. When, in reality, my daughters and my wife all seriously think I'm really very smart. In fact, they frequently need to defend themselves against me because they think I am making *them* feel stupid. It's frickin' crazy how this works . . .

My sister and I talked about her shame and how she perhaps was generating conflict with me where none existed—she was expecting that I too was ashamed of her the way she was ashamed of herself. It was an eye-opening experience for me to see what I was doing to others happening in reverse, so to speak.

She then hits me with the big question at the heart of it all: *"What am I supposed to do, Rick? I'm so ashamed, and I don't know how to fix it.* I don't know how to stop it." She then proceeded to sum up shame as it's understood in the biblical context. *"This is hell,"* she said. "This is hell on earth."

"Hell," as frequently defined in the Christian worldview, is an eternal separation from God. According to the story, hell, also termed "death" perhaps, found its way into human history as Adam heard God coming through the Garden in the cool of the day, and he hid. Shame-generating separation from God and separation from each other is the biblical definition of hell, and my sister knew that without even having all my advanced degrees in ministry!!

> *She then proceeded to sum up shame as it's understood in the biblical context. "This is hell"...*

Again, I'm not attempting to convince anyone of the historical validity of the Genesis account, but simply finding the dramatic irony in the fact that this concept—global and all-inclusive as it is—arrives announced early in the foundational book of three long-warring major world religions, and my sister and I are living it out over the phone years later.

Ironically, each of these religions, *afraid they are not enough* like all individuals and other institutions, have spent centuries warring against each other to arrive at some sort of self-validation, to be viewed as more "enough" than the others. This is very similar to what was predicted in Genesis 4 between the brothers warring for God's attention, Cain and Abel. We've evidently known about this issue and its ramification since the dawn of time, yet we continue to fall into the same old traps!

By the way, I don't want to forget that my sister asked the big question, "What am I supposed to do about this? How am I supposed to fix it?" The answer I gave her at the time was, "I don't know." As this book has alluded to already, I don't believe there is an easy fix at all, there's only a willingness to fight the battle every day and at every opportunity that presents itself. However, struck with the obviousness and magnitude of the dilemma, that's not how I answered in the moment.

How Big Is Yours? The Survival Question of Pastors

> *A great man is always willing to be little.*
> —Ralph Waldo Emerson

I was on my way to the bathroom at a Promise Keepers rally in the '90s. Promise Keepers was a Christian-based event that was supposed to instruct and encourage men on being followers of Jesus. I was probably only halfway out of my atheist place and was still attempting to understand what "following Jesus" was really all about, which made the irony of what I was about to experience even greater.

I got in line for the bathroom behind a couple of pastors, and the question they were discussing . . . on the way to the bathroom . . . was . . . "How big is yours?"

The Freudian irony wasn't lost on me, and I decided right then and there I had no interest in being a pastor and constantly have to compare the size of mine (congregation) with the size of my peers' (congregation). Fortunately, I later would learn I never needed to become a pastor—relieving me at least temporarily of that anxiety.

I was listening to Chuck Swindoll preach a sermon on the radio. Chuck had an uncanny way of keeping my attention on matters I otherwise found rather unbelievable. I think it was partially his voice, the tone and texture, but also the way he manipulated his speech so as to take me along with him as if riding some sort of water-based roller coaster. I'm not sure it would have mattered to me if Chuck had been describing the best way to gap a spark plug or the ideal path to find your way to heaven, I probably would have tuned in.

This particular day, something Chuck said caught my attention. I don't remember the context or the part of the Bible he was preaching from, but his point was clear, "If you can be happy doing anything else, *don't* become a pastor." I breathed a sigh of relief as it seemed I had many other interests occupying me at the time. However, my own shame drove my need to excel in every facet of my life and that would eventually include the church. The danger for me entering ministry was there from the beginning, I just wasn't aware of it at the time.

I remember going into my pastor's study one afternoon concerned about my ego. I went in to describe to the pastor that I felt like I had been climbing the corporate ladder in my company but that I had shifted the ladder, and now I was attempting to "climb the ladder" at church. I wondered what his thoughts were on that.

His response, "Well, at least your ladder is on the right wall."

I get the response. It was unsatisfactory to me even at that time largely because it didn't mesh with my understanding of Christianity—although I was prepared to believe there were things I didn't yet understand about Christianity.

According to Jesus, the leader of the Christian Church, the greatest shall be least and the least shall be the greatest. There is no need for a ladder going "up" at all, at least in his mind, as far as I can understand his mind. In theory, his physical demonstration of that was a ladder that brought him "down" to join humanity in all its weakness and limitations on earth. I'm not attempting to prove the value of Christianity but to show how quickly we will dismiss the realities of our own religion if it suits our ego.

The idea of climbing any ladder has shame-based concerns written all over it. Why did I have such a need to get ahead of everyone? Did it really matter what wall my ladder was on if it was pointing to some inner wound that needed to be addressed—my "not enoughness"? Or did it only matter that what was burning inside of me was a need to be recognized? A need to win? Maybe even a need to beat others and be known for beating others?

In the end, my own attempt at survival of the fittest (Christian) landed me 10 years later in another line. This time, it was while waiting to get the results of my psychological assessment before entering seminary, the school I would soon be attending to prepare to for ministry.

The intake data from that school suggests the vocation of "pastor" collects people with stronger-than-average narcissistic tendencies. My own seminary psychological prescreen assessment determined I was off the scale for narcissistic traits. Among the group of narcissists attempting to get into seminary the year I entered, I was leading the pack. Ironically, this was actually comforting to hear because I knew I was winning. However, it was actually a warning about how I would approach things in ministry but, more important, *why* I may be entering ministry to begin with.

At the time, I didn't care why I was doing what I was doing. I wish I did. I may have packed up right then and there realizing I had a lot of work to do before I thought about ministry—perhaps ministry wasn't the right place for me at all. But my narcissism was driving me there and the ladder had to reach someplace bigger than where I was.

Ironically, a good friend of mine was proofreading this book for me and stopped around this issue and remembered the time he specifically asked me why I decided to become a minister. He recalls me telling him the reason was because I "couldn't find one who was good." He brought back a flood of memories for me as I watched preacher after preacher and minister after minister thinking how I could do it better. Naïvely, I thought perhaps that was God calling me into ministry.

It's rather sobering looking at it in hindsight, that I might even claim God was on my side in all this. I can even remember expressing that to other people that maybe God was saying to me, "If you think you can do better, shut up and go do it." Now, 20 years later, I have a quote from Susan B. Anthony on my computer that says, "*I distrust people who know so well what God wants them to do, because*

> *What's clear about narcissism is that it ironically has less to do with self-love than it does with self-hatred and less to do with self-certainty and more to do with self-doubt.*

I notice it always coincides with their own desires."

Perhaps God did say to me, "Shut up and do it yourself if you think you can do better." But if he did, it was apparently more to bring me into an awareness that I couldn't do it better and/or to make me aware of what was really going on inside myself. Regardless, the issue of my narcissism was left at the table after my consultation with the prescreen psychologist with the assurance from me that "I could handle it."

At the time, my only translation of narcissism was "egotistical" or "self-centered"—terms that I didn't entirely see in myself. Because pastors could never be such things, I chose to use the more positively nuanced translation of high "self-esteem" or "self-confidence" and considered it more of a compliment than a warning. My translation brought little argument from the psychologist charged with reviewing my scores with me.

What's clear about narcissism is that it ironically has less to do with self-love than it does with self-hatred and less to do with self-certainty and more to do with self-doubt. These are shame issues we don't expect to find in people who appear "egotistical" or "full of themselves." However, shame is the underbelly of the egotistical personality, and the greater the ego, the more the hidden ugliness that person is attempting to cover up.

One of the books I read during my doctoral studies recounted the technical description of the narcissistic personality disorder (Capps 1993, 12–20) and appeared to have taken his list from my personal list of "issues."

1.   Hypersensitivity to the evaluation of others
2.   Lack of empathy from an early age
3.   Fantasies of unlimited success, power, brilliance, beauty, or ideal love
4.   Ambition that cannot be satisfied
5.   Interpersonal exploitation: others are used in order to achieve my ends; friendships are often made only after I consider how I can profit from them
6.   Effectiveness enhanced by drive for success, inhibited by a depression
7.   Unable to understand the complex emotional needs of other people
8.   Driven, pleasureless approach to goals
9.   Angry and resentful but concealing such beneath depressive moods
10. Feeling restless and bored when external glitter wears off
11. An experience of the lifelessness/emptiness of feelings that prompted counseling
12. Main task is to achieve the bliss/contentment of the primary narcissistic state
13. Not in danger of falling apart, but of depletion

It's a tough pill to swallow to consider that this list of personality traits applies to pastors in general and to myself in particular, but they frequently (usually?) do. This then gets combined with the shame pastors feel for understanding themselves to be this way when they should be able to rise above it. It certainly is not reflective of the person of Jesus Christ, the person pastors are emulating. Nonetheless, it's a snapshot of my own inner "woundedness."

Although the data suggest that seminary collects and trains the narcissistically wounded, it's been my experience that departments in denominations that start new churches sift off the ones wounded in ways that have become highly proficient with certain defense mechanisms such as productivity, perfectionism, legalism, and skills of manipulation, to name a few. Again, this person *looks* highly successful and would probably succeed equally well in corporate America, but is actually deeply wounded.

New church starting can actually feed the cravings of the wounded by knighting them denominational trendsetters in an attempt to keep them blazing rather than slowing down to ask themselves why being a trendsetter is so vital to their self-understanding. New church development can encourage those narcissistically wounded to continue to attempt to feed their wounds as they always have in the past. It's been my experience that "new church development" gives those most possessed with monument building the greatest and freshest opportunity to do so.

The Hunt for (Emotional) Food

When recognition is specific and deliberately delivered, it is even more motivating than money (Achor 2011, 58).

Corporate manipulation of individuals to meet the needs of the organization is a well understood tool of nearly every institution. After returning to corporate America, I was approached at a sales meeting by a very successful but rather intoxicated salesperson. He was about to land a pretty big piece of business—one that had been tough for a lot of people to crack. When that new piece of business began rolling in, it was quite certain he would make a significant amount of money through the company's sales incentive program. But he was still mad, or hurt.

"Not one person looked me in the eye, Rick. Not one person looked me in the eye and said 'great job.' Not one person could look me in the eye and just acknowledge what I had done, what I had accomplished. Yeah, I'll get the money," he said, "but what I want is the recognition. What I want is just that *one* person to look me in in the eye [he kept repeating this 'look me in the eye' phrase] and appreciate me and what I've done." Whether he really was under-appreciated by his employer, I don't know. What I do know is that same story is told at sales meetings across the country, across industries, and across racial and gender lines.

Across the country, a different young salesperson came up to me at another sales meeting. He too was drunk (by the way, I love going to sales meetings where people are drinking—it really is the truth serum), and he wanted to thank me.

He said, "You probably don't even remember what you did." This, by the way, is a statement of shame. I may or may not have remembered (I actually did in this case), but his insistence that I would forget came from his self-understanding that he was rather forgettable. It's unfortunate that his gauge of his self-worth is my memory!! Anyway, he said, "You probably don't even remember what you did, but at last year's district meeting, you toasted me and the success I had that year winning business." At this point, he, pretending to be me, raised his glass and said in a loud me-like voice, "To Stan." That was it. "To Stan."

He continued, "Rick, I spent my career with that customer to win that business. I lost my marriage to win that business. I sacrificed all that to win that piece of business, and not one person offered me as much as a toast. Rick," he said, "you gave that to me."

Now, again, I'm sure Stan made a ton of money that year, and maybe even received words of thanks from the company, I don't know. But if he did receive those words of thanks, what I do know is they never registered. Two things registered: he sacrificed a lot, and no one said thanks. Whether or not that's true, I can't confirm. But it certainly was his impression and a fairly deeply held impression, too. To hold on to that story for over a year, something pretty deep must have been going on.

Back again to the other side of the country, different bar, different sales rep, same story. He was explaining to me about what motivated him. "I don't give a #$#&! about the money; I want a Champions award [the name given to a select group of salespeople each year who succeed at the highest possible financial level]. It's true for everyone in this room," he said, motioning with his hand to a room full of salespeople drinking, talking, and otherwise letting off steam. "Ask any one of them—that's all anyone cares about—winning a Champions award."

There are a number of great "why" questions hidden here.

- **Why would someone sacrifice their marriage for accolades from work?**
- **Why would someone care more about a plastic award on a stand than what they get paid?**
- **Why would a couple of words from a coworker be the only thing a person remembers about their success?**

These stories could go on and on for volumes in almost any company, anywhere, likely since the dawn of time.

To me, this is one of two great mysteries behind the power of recognition (I'll get to the second in a moment).

The first is this: money is what we need to survive. It is the means by which we gain food, clothing, and shelter, to name the basic elements of our existence. It also pays our kids' tuition, mows the grass, allows us to travel, and propagates the species. Money is actually the core vehicle that we need for material survival.

Yet, what matters to us more than our material survival is our psychological survival. I would suggest that we all know that no matter how much money we have, if we are psychologically dead, we are just as dead although our lungs take in air and our hearts continue to beat. We all know the phrase that money can't buy happiness. I will add the concluding suggestion "but ego strokes can help."

Money *can* be what feeds our psychological survival. It may be the thing that prevents us from looking into the darkness of our limitations. This can be especially true if we have a lot of it such that we can be fooled into thinking we are superhuman. How much money we have can certainly also get us a comparative measure on where we are versus our neighbors. However, as we all know, comparison is a game without end.

None of us is likely to die from lack of money. However, lack of money may communicate something to our broken sense of self and act as a constant reminder that we are not enough—that we don't measure up—which can bring with it a certain type of "death" as well.

This brings us to the second important lesson here.

I remember my preaching professor describing being offered the role of head pastor at the largest congregation in the area. He was told that he was enthusiastically accepted by a vote of the congregational leadership 100:2, a vote "in favor" of a person to a scale unprecedented in the history of the congregation.

After his first sermon, as the congregants were shaking his hand on the way out of the sanctuary, all he could wonder was which two voted against bringing him to the church. With each handshake, he recalls asking in his head, "Was it you?"

Not only is it commonly understood that people are more motivated by recognition than by money, it's also commonly understood that it takes three positive affirmations to offset one negative experience. In fact, Achor's *The Happiness Advantage* says that research has actually determined the exact ratio!

2.9013 is the ratio of positive to negative interactions necessary to make a corporate team successful. This means it takes about three positive comments, experiences, or expressions to fend off the languishing effects of one negative (Achor 2011, 60).

Why aren't they one for one? If I say one bad thing to you, why can it not be offset by saying one good thing to you? This makes no mathematical sense without understanding what drives all of humanity: shame.

Corporate entities know this and successfully use rewards, awards, and recognition (private and public) because they know it's necessary to get results and to pay the least amount of money to get people to stay. If we weren't repeatedly hearing the voice telling us we are not enough, would we make the same decisions about what church we attend or what company we work for? I don't think so.

Shame allows us to be manipulated by our company, our spouse, our kids, our friends, and our inner voice to do things that are frequently not in our best interest—things that are frequently harmful to us or people with which we come into contact. It's surprising to me how easily I can find myself swayed by attention from people in power—from my supervisors or my peers or people who want to get something from me. The most frequent way they can do that is to play to my inner sense of self-doubt by telling me I'm great. If I really knew I was great, I wouldn't need their words and could make my own decisions. Even Sigmund Freud knew he could be swayed by this power!

When someone abuses me, I can defend myself. But against praise, I am defenseless. —Sigmund Freud

Early in my career, I was a fairly new employee with my company and quickly learned how important it was to procure samples of competing products. Ideally, you'd go about getting that sample by asking your customer for it, but everyone knew that rarely happened. It was never verbalized that a sample should be "stolen," but the recognition you received for obtaining one garnered special praise.

Shortly after starting with my first employer in the early 1990s, I was in a paper mill in Michigan and seized the opportunity. I had the sample. It was in my briefcase. All I had to do was leave. But I couldn't do it.

I wish I could say I was wracked with moral guilt for my deed, but I wasn't. I wish I could confess to asking myself, "What would Jesus do?" but I didn't. I was afraid of getting caught. I wasn't afraid of getting in trouble either; I was afraid of being exposed for the thief I was. I was more afraid of the shame it would generate in me if the truth were to be discovered about me (that I was a thief) than I was by the potential for recognition, the reward I would receive, to soothe my shame. The potential for pain was greater than the potential for pleasure even though the odds of getting caught were miniscule. It grieves me to say that the church can stumble in similar ways.

GOTTA FEED THE MACHINE

I was having lunch with a local pastor after having attended his congregation's worship service a couple times prior that same month. We were discussing ministry and ministry views. Personally, I was feeling jealous of how he was able to grow a church so effectively when I was seemingly unable to keep mine functional from week to week. I guess I was caught up body and soul in the "How big is yours?" conversation I had dreaded years before.

He was a great speaker and even better worship leader, a true showman (and I say that in the best possible way). I could see why people were attracted to his congregation (even though we were similarly gifted, or so I thought). I asked him if he ever took a break, gave lesser talented people an opportunity to lead to train them up as future church leaders.

He liked the idea but would never do it on big Sundays such as Christmas or Easter. He wanted to make sure the most effective people were at the helm when there was the greatest likelihood of new potential members. I challenged whether this wasn't somewhat manipulative. Something like a bait and switch where you put the top entertainers in front on the big Sundays hoping people would come back only to eventually need to fill in with the less-entertaining folks on following weekends.

Then he made a comment I will never forget. It was a truth I had experienced myself but never heard it spoken so directly, *"You gotta feed the machine."*

> *The Christian church, the one institution that shouldn't be afraid of death (since we believe in life after death), was fighting for survival with the rest of the created order.*

At that point, I realized that the pressure to do what you have to do to survive—even in the church—can be overwhelming. The Christian church, the one institution that shouldn't be afraid of death (since we believe in life after death), was fighting for survival with the rest of the created order. The church, whose primary motivation you would think should be a voice alarming us against being manipulated by shame, is frequently walking lock-step with all the other institutions in the world fighting for survival.

I recently received a form donation request from a denominational leader via email. After discussing the great cause I would be supporting with my donation and the importance of acting now as time was running out, he thanked me and added the following postscript.

> *P.S. If you haven't received the note I mailed you, the Covenant Circle is a group of [denominational] pastors, retired pastors, and surviving spouses who support the ministry of [our denomination] by giving at least $100 annually to [our denomination's] Ministry Fund. If you decide to join, we'll recognize you in our annual report.*

It was the last line that caught my attention. I wanted to give more after I read that last line. Maybe that's just me but I don't think it is. I think it was a form suggested by consultants who know people will give more if they know they will be recognized. What they may not know is that they are manipulating a person's sense of shame for their own institution's advantage.

As Christians, Jesus has taught us that what we do generously we should such that even our right hand does not know what our left hand is doing. The idea here is so we do our good deeds without mixed motives. However, this last line in the email assures me, a Christian, that I will get recognized for my good deed. This is sadly necessary in our culture because the best way to get people to do what you want is to promise them recognition for their greatness.

This is similar to the flood of stories I get from salespeople in our organization who are so willing to sacrifice so deeply—not for money, but for recognition—and not because they are egotistical and think highly of themselves but because they are ashamed and are afraid they are not enough. It's also a root reason I ended up attempting to go into ministry to begin with.

A Champion Among Champions

"Do you want to sell sugar water for the rest of your life, or do you want to come with me and change the world?" —What Steve Jobs said to Pepsi executive John Sculley to lure him to Apple (Bloomberg TV 2010)

I was standing in the kitchen of the home where I grew up after just announcing to my parents that I was going to be headed back to college—seminary, actually. I told them I was going to get a master's degree in ministry. My mom was surprised and made a very reasonable reflection, "But you don't like people." This should have tipped me off that there was a problem with my plan for pursuing this degree. She was right, of course, but I wasn't slowing down to take a look at myself, as I had greatness to achieve.

My dad intuitively figured that this would be the end of my successful and high-paying foray into corporate America and asked an equally reasonable question, "Why?"

As you know from the beginning of this book, this is the main question that needed to be asked. My motives needed to be challenged, and this was a question of motives. Evidently, my dad didn't realize that recognition was more important to me than money—or maybe he didn't see how a lowly job in the church gave near as much recognition as corporate America.

From my dad's perspective, I had never really had any religious inclinations, and we were not a very devout home—by the time we were in high school, we had stopped attending any church altogether. Not attending church was just fine by me; I had no use for something getting me up early on a Sunday morning when I had been out with my friends the night before.

So, what would make a fella give up good money and security to pursue such an endeavor? As you know from my previous discussion, to the wounded soul recognition is more important than money.

So, when my dad asked me "why" I was doing what I was doing, I told him it was a call to greatness and quoted the Steve Jobs words that lured Sculley from Pepsi. I told him I was tired of selling sugar water, and I wanted to change the world—I wanted to be great (ironically, I am now back to selling "sugar water"!!!).

Let's not miss the irony here. I wanted to be "great," so I was going into a religion where its leader (Jesus) had said, "The first shall be last and the greatest shall be least." Evidently, I wasn't actually paying attention to that part. I'm not entirely sure the church was paying sole attention to that part, either.

My issues would strike me powerfully in the face in 2002. I was at a denominational conference for pastors who were starting new churches. The conference title was called "Weekend of Champions." The idea was that we, the new church start pastors, were champions. The idea was a rush. The idea that I was now at the "weekend of champions" helped affirm that I was becoming "enough." I was something great. It soothed my wounded soul.

I don't believe this was a willful act of "manipulation," and I don't think there was any malice involved in the process whatsoever. However, I can't imagine Jesus handing out "weekend of champions" T-shirts to his disciples. What I do know is it felt good, it sure was motivating, and I believe all institutions that have done their homework know how motivating adoration can be.

The dilemma came the next day. A smaller group of people were asked to stand during the conference for special recognition. They were the "tent-making" pastors—the pastors who were still working outside the church so as to alleviate the financial burden on their congregation and the denomination. These people were literally anointed the "champions of champions."

Hot shame burst through my veins. I had completely funded myself going through seminary by remaining employed, while most of my colleagues became a drain (or so I perceived) on their congregations and the denomination. I remained employed in corporate America for the first two years while we were launching this ministry so I would not be a financial burden and so that the money of ministry wouldn't delude me into making decisions for purposes of retaining my salary.

I was a "champion of champions," yet I was unable to stand because several months prior, I had left my job and had begun taking a paycheck from the church to offset the challenges of raising a new houseful of adopted teenagers. I was devastated. I was not enough. I took the money. I wanted to be enough. I wanted to be more than enough. Perhaps I could prove my worth once my congregation became great. But in this moment, I did not make the leaders' board.

What I didn't realize about being a leader in the church would be taught to me soon enough by a now-renowned pastor who had faced identical challenges in his ministry. . .

If I succeed in getting anyone's attention, what I want to say is that the pastoral vocation is not a glamorous vocation and that Tarshish is a lie. Pastoral work consists of modest, daily, assigned work. It is like farm work. Most pastoral work involves routines similar to cleaning out the barn, mucking out the stalls, spreading manure, pulling weeds. This is not, any of it, bad work in itself, but if we expected to ride a glistening black stallion in daily parades and then return to the barn where a lackey grooms our steed for us, we will be severely disappointed and end up being horribly resentful (Peterson 1992, 16).

I was likely en route to a whole heaping portion of resentment and didn't see it coming.

Shame requires us to fight for our emotional food—validation that we somehow are enough. We hunt for it in nooks and crannies, under rocks, and in places we should never be or go.

AN INSATIABLE HUNGER FOR VALIDATION

Since beginning the process of writing this book, I've done something I swore I would never do: I opened a Facebook page. I've come to understand that it's vital in our world to be functional in the realm of social media in order to communicate your message.

I was having lunch with my oldest daughter Tilonda about that time (the one who believed she was the "ugly one"), and I asked her about this weird phenomenon I saw happening. It had to do with the selfie. For starters, I find it fascinating in a conversation about *shame* how many people are taking pictures of themselves. I don't entirely know how to process that reality but, of course, I have to wonder *why* they are doing that sort of thing.

Below any new selfie is the list of people who comment on the picture. If the picture is of a girl, people all comment "You're so beautiful" or "You are hot" or some such complimentary language. If it's a guy, the aim is similar like "You're a stud" or something. It was almost as if this process was the point of the posting—to get people to respond in affirming tones toward our appearance.

So, I asked my daughter what was going on there. She confessed that (in her opinion), that's exactly what people are doing. She said in one sense, it makes you feel good to post a really good picture of yourself and get positive comments back from people. She said it's all about making you feel good.

I asked her if, like my professor who was obsessed with the two people who didn't vote for him, if you ever get hurt by the number of positive comments being less than you hoped. I never saw any negative comments, but I realized sometimes there were 10 positive comments, and sometimes there were just two. I asked her if she ever felt bad when it was over, if you only get two positive comments instead of 10. I asked her if she wondered about whether people really thought you were beautiful or were only saying that hoping you would tell them they look beautiful on *their* Facebook.

Her response? Yes, to all. "It's a hot mess" (an interesting phrase I hear my daughters use a lot). She described a fight she got into with her younger sister Tapricia who accused her of posting pictures just for attention. She said she got so mad at her sister for saying that, and it generated a *huge* blowout between the two of them.

"But," she said, "you know what? She was right. That's why I was doing it. I was looking for affirmation and attention. Why do I have to do that, Rick? And why do I have to get into a big fight with my sister when she busts me for it, but she's actually right?"

As you know if you've read this far, "Why?" is the question indeed, and you also probably know my answer: Shame.

I'm sure that when this book goes onto Amazon or wherever it goes, I will be joining a throng of authors searching for reviews and stars that will help validate me as a person just like I search for the "likes" and "loves" I get whenever I post my own thoughts to Facebook.

The narcissistic personality—the shame-based personality—has an insatiable need for love, appreciation, and admiration from other people, an inability to develop relationships beyond what a person can "do" for them, and a complete revulsion for being known as a "loser" (the narcissist and shame-based person must always be a "winner").

If you believe the intake data from my seminary, many (most) pastors struggle with narcissistic tendencies. Capps even goes so far as to describe pastors as a group as "*mirror hungry*" (1993, 63). This could create a need in the modern pastor and congregation to gather as many people as possible to validate themselves and to be seen as a winner. A congregation then might transfer their need for approval and affirmation onto him/her with the pastor transferring his/her need for love and winning/losing onto them. It all has the potential for getting quite dysfunctional in a hurry. Frankly, it can become a "hot mess."

Pastors can struggle, then, with the internal battle of desperately wanting to be recognized while feeling deep shots of shame; they believe they ought to be able to live above such needs of admiration and affirmation (Capps 1993, 61). Even in corporate America where it is common knowledge that people are motivated more by praise and adulation (mirroring) than money, none will admit publicly that these needs exist—none will admit to being psychologically "needy." To do so is shameful—in the church, *or* corporate America, *or* even within your own soul.

> *In fact, asking why we are so deeply affected by negative comments actually generates more shame when we have to discover why we are so easily hurt.*

As I previously mentioned, an amazing number of people will describe to me the anger they feel when they are not recognized at work. Very few, however, are willing to wonder *why* they are so hurt in the core of their soul by an institution that is not designed to help them feel good about themselves but rather to give them a day's wage for a day's work. In fact, asking *why* we are so deeply affected by negative comments actually generates *more* shame when we have to discover why we are so easily hurt. For this reason, shame itself will prevent us from asking the question. It doesn't want to be discovered!

Frequently, unsatisfied with the love and admiration he/she is getting, a pastor struggling with his or her own narcissism may even then encourage their flock to evangelize in order to feed his/her hunger for love and fear of failure. The congregation can be eager to participate *or* can become resistant and resentful as it struggles with its own narcissistic tendencies and desires for the full attention of the pastoral and ministry staff. I can't recount the number of hurt congregants that are out there because the pastor didn't show up at his or her function.

The self-preservation anxiety felt in mainline denominations may also come into play here very much like it does in the business world. Church planting and evangelism are seen as truly the only mechanisms for denominational survival; the total weight of which can come down on and around the new church start pastor so afraid of losing and so in need of being the "champion."

With evangelism comes the ultimate testament to the pastor as a "winner." First, the building (the bigger, the better—Freud would have a great time with that one as well!). Second is the survival and continued relevance of an entire institution. The machine must be fed! Pretty soon, we're back in line for the bathroom at a Promise Keepers rally comparing ourselves to our fellow pastors.

Is it possible that today's pastoral model and congregational understanding is one that has evolved more out of our own disorder than biblical truth? Personally, I'd never foreseen the forces that had moved me in this direction; forces I now attribute as much to my own psychological issues as any call from God.*

Now, please hear me here. Evangelism (communication of the good news of Jesus Christ) is a hugely important biblical principle, but the motive for the evangelism is what I question. Is it so that the pastor will be seen as a "winner" or so that the evangelist might experience what Christ experienced: rejection, acceptance, and

---

* Though I'm prepared to consider psychology as a means through which the spirit of God may conduct his business of "calling."

persecution as they headed into the harvest fields? It seems to me, we Christians are called much more frequently and intently to "follow him" than to "win souls."

The problem for me and our congregation was that, in the absence of growth, large congregational size, or monuments of success, there was no adequate mirror. This can be debilitatingly shame generating for a narcissistic pastor. When I stood with other pastors on the way to the urinal, I would have to defend why mine was so small.

Ultimately, it was one issue that drove me from ministry: I could no longer stand seeing myself manipulate people to get what I wanted to make a church successful. That, of course, and the F bombs I dropped on those congregants who rolled their eyes at me. I'm sure that didn't help, either.

You Can Even Fool Yourself: The Cloud of Motivations

The closing of the congregation I launched was intensely shame generating. It reinforced the reality that I was, indeed, "not enough." Since that time, I've realized I have attempted in numerous ways to reprove to myself and the world that I *am* enough. I needed to overcome the shame of that first church loss. Now, more than ever, I need to prove to the world that I can do something significant. My fear is that this book may be another such attempt as well. The question, again, needs to be "why" I need to write.

I always believed I had a book in me. I always felt like it was something I wanted to do. The problem is, I always felt that way for the same reasons I went into ministry—I felt like I had something to say that people needed to hear. Why I always believe I have something to say that people need to hear is a good question. I suppose I kind of think we all do. However, the undergirding fear in that is that even if I *didn't* have something to say, that that didn't make me "bad." Perhaps you know that about yourself. I'm not sure I know it about myself. So, in the midst of the conundrum about what to do now that I was no longer in ministry, I was offered an opportunity to join a publishing program that would lead and coach me through the process of writing.

I was perusing the news on MSN. Like many news channels on the internet, the bottom is filled with sponsored links, which I rarely hit. This time, one caught my eye. It was a link featuring an interview of a well-known author on how to be a successful author. I watched and found it fascinating. The catch? I would certainly have to pay money to join the program.

The flags immediately went up. I knew this Siren song calling my shame to the craggy cliffs of destruction. My sore, wounded soul wanted to be famous—

> *My sore, wounded soul wanted to be famous—especially after the failure of ministry. It needed to be soothed with the prestige of having a book—a popular book—and it seemed an easy step to pay someone to get me there.*

especially after the failure of ministry. It needed to be soothed with the prestige of having a book—a popular book—and it seemed an easy step to pay someone to get me there.

I declined, and I tried to quit watching the videos, which were now inundating my inbox.

I was afraid that my desire to get my message out was the voice of my inner critic telling me I was not enough. I was equally afraid that my desire to not invest in my message was also steeped in the voice of my inner critic telling me not to be a fool again, not to be so arrogant, not to be such a stupid #$^!@ idiot. I asked myself what I would do if I were truly not afraid. This had to be my motivating force.

In the end, I took the leap. I spent the money. I joined the program. I wrote this book. The outcomes, motivations, and desire to not be drawn again into fear are still questions yet to be answered. I fight daily with attempting to find my greatness in being the least of these—it's a concept I almost can't fathom. The temptation to feel the fleeting validation of fame is fierce and makes me want to run for the exits even though it's the very thing my heart seems to desire. The one thing I know for sure is that this battle against my own motives is one I share with every other human out there!! I am not alone.

Once you start trying to face and cope with this conflict in your life—understanding why we do what we do—you must take seriously how this particular type of warfare is both spiritual and psychological and is consistent with the entire human experience, it's part of what being human is and means.

> *It matters not if the person earns a two-comma salary or works for minimum wage. She may be married or single. He may be African American or Caucasian. Depressed, anxious or just plain angry; happy or sad or indifferent. He may be the father or the son, the employer or the employee. It maybe an individual, a couple, family, community, school or business organization. And you needn't have ever darkened the office door of a psychiatrist. It doesn't require the breakdown of our mental health to be plagued with it. It only requires that you have a pulse. To be human is to be infected with this phenomenon we call shame.* —Curt Thomson (2015, 21)

WE'VE ALL BEEN HIT BY THE SAME WINDMILL

> *I have never met anyone who did not have a struggle with it. I have met a lot of people who didn't think they did* (Moore 2003, 144).

I was offered the windmill phrase by my friend from the Netherlands during a visit one summer. We were describing the way we're all sort of messed up in sort of the same way, just with different symptoms. It may be the Dutch version of what they were trying to get at in Genesis with the snake—trying to show us that these issues found their way into our very first ancestors and just keep coming.

SEAT 17C

Flying from Little Rock to Chicago, I didn't realize I would soon be struck with gratitude. It's not an emotion I experience frequently; I think it's part of being so blessed with such a strongly narcissistic personality.

Normally, I'm grateful when no one is sitting next to me. That usually is worthy of handstands. It's then I think God is really looking out for me. If someone *must* sit next to me, I hope they are small and quiet. Well, today in seat 17C, I would get the "small" part anyway, but not the quiet.

I have no idea what her name was, but she was bubbly and happy. She was the kind of person who makes me wonder the "hows and whys" of what makes someone that way. She was chatty and smiley, and I had to know what was up.

She didn't seem put off by my grilling her on what made her tick. She didn't know the extent to which I was struggling with my own depression, the way darkness hung on me, or the way anxiety was filling my soul.

She didn't know self-doubt and self-contempt filled my spirit. She didn't know I referred to myself as "stupid, f***ing, piece of sh*t."

She gave me some cursory responses explaining how she's so happy and bubbly—typical stuff you would hear from someone in their mid-twenties, I guess. She focuses on the positive. She always looks for the upside of situations. Quite frankly, she tells me, she loves her job, and she just had a really, really, great week doing a photo shoot in Little Rock.

I did quiz her a little about what she did on the photo shoot as she did me on where I work. I described to her that they made a lot of paper in Little Rock and how I worked at paper mills. In particular, I helped chemical sales engineers at the paper mills understand how to deliver value to their customer, making packaging grades of paper utilizing our chemistry and practices to improve . . . blah blah blah blah . . . and I looked at her and I said, "I can't believe how boring that was after actually hearing those words come out of my mouth."

She appeared interested. Or she was kind. I don't know which. She graciously said it was very nice to talk with me but that she was going to zone out for a while. Ha! I said to myself. I'd become "that guy." I'd become the guy that chats the ear of the person next to me. I'd become the guy I hate sitting by.

She drifted off into her book, and I pulled out my laptop to attempt to catch up on some work.

That's when she tapped my shoulder.

"I want to change my answer," she said.

Being old and weak of mind, I couldn't honestly remember the question.

"OK," I said. "I'll think about it. What you got?"

"It's gratitude," she said. "That's why I'm happy."

From there, I can't remember how many twists and turns the conversation took. I don't know if I was talking more or listening more. I wanted to be listening, but the more she talked, the more I had to say.

Ironically, she confessed she was full on self-contempt. A comrade I found with my own soul, but I was confused at the same time. How could someone so happy be filled with self-contempt?

Specifically, she described her fear of being "seen" and her concern for what people thought of her. She said she was overly concerned with *how* she was presented to people, specifically how she was introduced. She was concerned with things of shame just like the rest of humanity I've come across. I wish I could say I felt bad for her, but I think I was too busy feeling better for myself that shame truly found itself even in the happiest of people.

We talked about the church. She told me of her time in a Catholic university where it was discovered that she'd not been baptized. She told of me of the shame and the conflicting love she had for attending Catholic mass. Obviously, not being baptized, she couldn't actually participate in communion, but she loved the experience of it. But she remembered sitting alone in the pew as people went forward to receive communion. Ultimately, that's what shame does, leaves us sitting alone in the pew.

I spoke of Jesus and of the entrance of shame into the world in Genesis. She appeared engrossed in the conversation. I say "appeared" because I couldn't tell if her engagement was a projection of my own engagement or was sincere on her part. I wish I would have listened more instead of talking. I know what *I* think. That's part of the problem with shame, we tend to get much-needed reinforcement from speaking, from being the "expert" and less from listening. Shame actually prevents good listening.

I found myself wanting to tell this young gal's story. I found myself wanting to tell the church about this young gal and how she wanted to be part of them but was too ashamed. How did that happen?

I gave her my card, hoping she would contact me again so I could somehow record all the experiences her young 24 years offered me. The list of action items on her phone calendar she made to attack her shortcomings—resentment is the one I remember clearest—was an interesting trick. However, I remember the fear of abandonment the clearest because this is actually a root fear of shame. We are afraid that when we and our shortcomings are exposed, we will be abandoned. Infantile as it sounds, it's reality. She was just able to articulate it.

As the plane began its descent, I realized I was being severely hampered by the altitude shift affecting my ability to hear out of my left ear. It was getting harder and harder to hear what she was saying, but it was becoming more and more important that I capture every word. I strained and struggled to grab what I could, all while being certain that I missed so much. We parted company with a handshake as I went to the board to see when my flight to Kalamazoo was leaving, and she headed for the exits.

Then, sitting at an airport restaurant in O'Hare, having been talked out of the comfort of my Bud Light and into a Weihenstephaner (a Belgian beer) by my very skilled waiter, I realized again that she is everyone.

While I wanted to make sure I accurately recorded my conversation with her for the betterment of others, I realized that I could pick up where I left off with anyone in this airport at any time who could tell me their own tale of shame and self-improvement if they were people who had been willing to plumb those depths to the extent of the 24-year-old lady sitting in seat 17A.

> *I could pick up where I left off with anyone in this airport at any time who could tell me their own tale of shame and self-improvement*

What has become the truest irony in all this is that the gal in 17A was reading Brené Brown's book I mentioned in my preface, *The Gifts of Imperfection*, which I now quote routinely. Some call that serendipity. Some call it karma. Some call it God. I call it "we're all in this together." She insisted I take her copy. I have since bought my own and recommend it to you as well.

CHAPTER 4

Symptoms of the Disease

We are all infected with a spiritual disease. Its name is shame
(Thomson 2015).

There are many analogies I've used for shame that all seem to fit certain niches, even though no single analogy fits perfectly. For example, already I have used the ideas of snake venom and a bus to help understand this thing going on inside us. I have also used the idea of disease, particularly naming shame as a virus at the heart of the disease. The thing about diseases we all know is that we find them when patients begin to present certain symptoms.

The challenge is coming up with a strategy to attack the disease and not the symptom.

You've certainly already noticed a couple of my "symptoms" of the virus in my soul. You don't have to look beyond the lump in

> *The challenge is coming up with a strategy to attack the disease and not the symptom.*

my hand to know one of my symptoms is rage. Although I'm certain there is probably some benefit to anger management classes to help me cope with the symptom of my shame—much like taking an aspirin for a head-ache—*unless you understand the root reason for the headaches, they will return or require constant medication.* Although the path of constant medication is increasingly popular and, quite frankly a path I'm still attempting to find myself, the goal should be to find a way to live with the virus that doesn't require heavy sedation.

Symptoms can also appear to be polar opposites, but the source is the same. For example, just consider a couple of people at my gym.

One morning, there was a guy getting dressed in the locker room after his workout. He always uses the same locker and always gets dressed in the same place—in front of the mirror. It's actually the same place he always works out. When he walks from machine to machine, he doesn't look forward to see where he's going but looks to his side so he can watch himself walking to his next station in the mirror.

The other person is the frump. This person is hiding behind as many baggy clothes as possible. They never raise their head, and they have a deep aversion to looking in the mirror at all for fear of what they will see. They hate mirrors and, given a chance, can probably detail for you every aspect of what is wrong with their body and their appearance.

At the surface, these appear to be people with two very different issues when, in reality, they have very different symptoms of the same issue. Shame.

The irony of shame is it can get us to want to preach from the mountaintops in an attempt to get the admiration our soul needs. It can just as easily get us to shut down and never speak a word for fear of looking like an idiot. That's why it can be so challenging to diagnose the symptoms of shame because they can frequently look like they (the symptoms) are coming from very opposite places.

...when it comes to shame, the symptoms are actually modes of self-defense.

Today, I still hear a voice demanding my greatness be recognized. However, after experiencing the shame of the congregation falling apart, this voice is now trying to protect me from my grandiosity by telling me to just shut the hell up.

The key is to see that *when it comes to shame, the symptoms are actually modes of self-defense.*

There are any number of shame-based modes of self-defense the scope of which John Bradshaw does a great job detailing that I will not be able to do here. However, symptoms/strategies are largely broken into two categories: strategies of defense and strategies of transfer (Kaufman 1992, 81). These are what we show the world as "symptoms" of the shame disease boiling about underneath such that a symptom and a defense mechanism are the same thing.

The point I do want to hit upon from Bradshaw is that these defense strategies (or "scripts" as he calls them) are what will lead to our destructive decisions.

A person with internalized shame believes he is inherently flawed, inferior and defective. Such a feeling is so painful that defending scripts (or strategies) are developed to cover it up. These scripts are the roots of violence, criminality, war, and all forms of addiction (Bradshaw 2005, 4).

Defense strategies function in a way as evidence of what's brewing inside me (such as the word "symptom" might imply), but they exist beyond just evidence, they are symptoms with a function. Their function is to throw people (including myself) off the trail of the *real* issue.

"A person begins to develop strategies of defense against experiencing shame and strategies for the interpersonal transfer of experienced shame. Strategies of defense are essentially forward-looking; they aim at protecting the self against further exposure to any future experiences of shame" (Kaufman 1992, 81). These are what I developed at the earliest age as I concocted a false self to project for the world to see, so the "real me" wasn't out there, exposed to the embarrassing pain of shame.

A fig leaf covering is a great example here as well.

Genesis 3 [7] Then the eyes of both of them were opened, and they realized they were naked; so they sewed fig leaves together and made coverings for themselves.

Shame (the *fear* of being exposed) is now an integral part of the human experience, and the reaction is obvious: hide—it's a symptom and a defense mechanism. As I mentioned earlier, this is what Adam did in the garden when God came looking for him; he felt fear *specifically because he was naked,* so he hid. He didn't want to be seen naked before God. That is shame. That's what shame causes to happen in us. And it requires us to come up with a means for covering our nakedness—our vulnerability—our exposure to ridicule and potential abandonment and the *pain* associated with that. In a group meeting of any kind, that can equally present itself as the wallflower who won't make a peep during the entire event and the other person who won't shut up.

> *Shame (the fear of being exposed) is now an integral part of the human experience, and the reaction is obvious: hide.*

We've also called this your "false self"—that person you project for people to prevent them from knowing who you really are. For me, it was important to project an assertive, outgoing, self-confident image, even though every recollection I had as a child was one of fear and insecurity—feelings that, as far as I could tell, stayed with me at least through high school. Volumes have been written on the false-self—its production and ramifications—and is a subject that has been dealt with extensively.

Rage was the "strategy of defense" I had chosen to use when I felt shame from my daughter or my congregants rolling their eyes at me or even when I attacked myself in the field after not properly tying my shoes! But I'm sure it also helped me transfer some of the shame onto others, as well. Perhaps I was hopeful that my daughter would have felt bad for me breaking my hand instead of the indifference she rightly chose.

The problem with rage, as Kaufman points out (1992, 84), is that it's toxic. If it's allowed to ferment, it can transition into other symptoms, ranging from bitterness to resentfulness and, in myself, a brewing self-hatred since there weren't enough entities in the world for me to unload the vastness of my rage upon. Rage can appear as a spirit of constant criticism or cynicism as well. None of these things are significant contributors to an enjoyable life, but they will probably protect you from being exposed.

All these defense strategies will drive people away from you before those same people *choose* to leave you when they find out who you really are. This outcome is *far* more advantageous because somehow, your subconscious knows they aren't really leaving you—they are leaving who you project. It's the same reason we can't accept praise from people for things our false self has done either; we know it's not us they are praising.

This was one of my fears all along with my daughter who wanted me to hate her and the way she acted toward me. My fear was that if I gave in and acted in a hateful way, it would have achieved her shame's end-game—somehow keeping me at a distance so there would never be a danger of me abandoning her. You also routinely hear of people attempting to drive away spouses for whom they don't feel worthy. It happens every day.

Narcissism (egotism/self-centeredness), for me, was also a form of self-defense. It served (and is still serving, to an extent) to protect me from being vulnerable and exposed and prevented me from being "discovered" for who I am.

Like most people, I didn't have a conscious understanding of what was going on at the time. In fact, one frequently quoted definition of being a narcissist is not being willing or able to acknowledge you are one (my refusal to hear my condition from the psychologist who screened me going into seminary is a good example here).

What's interesting about narcissism is that it's not typically a "direct attack" sort of defense but is still one that can be particularly harmful to the person afflicted with it—a demonstration of how self-defense quickly becomes self-sabotage. It may not have a direct impact on the lives of people around the narcissist as much as something like blame unless they *too* are using narcissism as *their* defense, in which case it becomes quite a show.

I was doing a radio interview and had been asked about how I went from being an atheist to an ordained minister. I first had described the process of becoming an atheist to begin with—which was quite an ordeal. But when I paused to look for some feedback, the radio host went on a 10-minute rant about the time he had spent in Russia and the atheism that's rampant there and what he did about it and blah blah blah. All of which was very interesting, but it was clear this fella didn't want to hear my story at all but was simply waiting to tell his.

The striving for power is a direct attempt to compensate for the sense of defectiveness which underlies internalized shame.

Evidently, there's only so much attention that can be paid to any one person in the room at any given time and watching a narcissist demanding it all becomes an excruciating experience for your fellow narcissists in the room who also want part of the action. I've heard it said that if you want to assess how egotistical or narcissistic *you* are, see how much *someone else's* egotism bugs you!!

Related to my own experience with narcissism in general is what Kaufman calls "striving for power"—which you've seen frequently, as I've told my own story.

"The striving for power is a direct attempt to compensate for the sense of defectiveness which underlies internalized shame . . . to the degree that one is successful in gaining power, particularly over others, one becomes increasingly less vulnerable to further shame. This is so because shame usually travels down the dominance hierarchy . . . this person is also well suited for transferring blame" (Kaufman 1992, 85).

A Special Shout Out to Perfectionism

Research shows that perfectionism hampers success. In fact, it's often the path to depression, anxiety, addiction, and life paralysis (Brown 2010, 56).

As I mentioned, there is an infinite number of symptoms for this one condition and this book is not large enough to go into all of them. However, one of the most toxic and popular is perfectionism, which itself has a wide array of variants. For example, if you were to look at my desk, you would be quite certain I was *not* a perfectionist. However, there is a difference between being detail oriented and being a perfectionist. Perfectionism is a front, a projection, a picture we want to portray of ourselves not only to others but to ourselves as well.

In February of 2009, I stood over the frozen body of yet another dead calf. I had decided (based on advice from others) to move my calving to the winter. This had proven to be a miserable disaster. I lost six or seven calves that year. This cow I had checked every couple of hours because it was brutally cold out. She had been in the barn but was showing no signs of calving so I let her out for the night. By 5 am she had had her calf. Apparently, she had calved up beside a gate and had squirted the calf under the gate and outside the pasture. That's where it lay. Frozen solid.

I raged against myself and my idiocy for not checking more often or for deciding to calve in the winter at all. My incompetence had directly led to the death of all these calves. My knowledge of animal husbandry was clearly imperfect, and the results were literally piling up on me.

Each time a calf died, my perfectionism forced me to take it personally. I always felt like such a complete idiot and loser whenever I lost one, assuming there was something I should have known or done to prevent it from happening. Perfectionism prevents you from being OK with making mistakes even though making them is just what humans do. Perfectionism's goal is to lift you above being human at all, period. This, as we know, is an exercise in futility.

The reason I think perfectionism is such a powerful defense strategy is because it gets at the root issue of shame so quickly. The voice of shame is reminding you that you are not enough, and the perfectionist is going about doing whatever is necessary to make sure they are (enough). Unlike rage or contempt, which can hurt other people, perfectionism is geared almost entirely at self-destruction. It is also the strategy that is most easily understood as being doomed to fail because perfection is humanly unattainable.

The myth you're living under if you're using this defense strategy is that when you attain perfection, you will no longer be at risk for experiencing shame. The myth, of course, is that arriving at perfection is possible at all. It then spawns ugly twin siblings known as comparison and competitiveness. These twins, ironically, are always eventually shame-*generating* endeavors, although they are designed to be part of what prevents us from experiencing that pain!!

Remember too that one of shame's goals is to remain hidden. A coworker commented that her perfectionism actually distracted her from addressing her shame. She would spend so much time striving, working, comparing, and competing that she couldn't address *why* she was doing such things. "It [the reason for her perfectionism] never went anywhere," she said. "I just got distracted from it."

It is the *hidden* driver behind our destructive decisions . . .

This leads to the problem of comparison. Theodore Roosevelt, one of the most accomplished men in U.S. history, coined the phrase, "Comparison is the thief of joy." It's something of a relief to think that even a man as historic as Theodore Roosevelt would struggle with comparing himself to others.

It seems like comparison would be a helpful thing. A buddy of mine from high school insisted that the way he looked at life was under the awareness that "it could always be worse." That helped him live in gratitude for what he had and with compassion for those who had less. He, unlike me, was very compassionate. That said, he also spent a great deal of time as a raging alcoholic so I guess we *do* all have our own defense mechanisms.

However, for a perfectionist, comparison is indeed the thief of joy because you, for whatever weird reason, can *only* see those who are outperforming you. Those are the only images your inner critic will allow to get into your data processing center. It's important that your inner critic not let you see anyone *under*performing you because then you might stop your striving for perfection. This then opens you up to the possibility of feeling the pain of shame and, remember, that's the critic's job, to prevent that from happening.

Although my friend from high school was able to look at those less fortunate than he was and feel a sense of gratitude for what he did have in life, it's also equally likely that we will look at those "beneath us" and get a sense of relief that "we are not like that." That's shame talking as well. That's the inner voice in one sense trying to soothe your own soul too. But its next message may be an attempt to usher up some defense to get you to do something to prevent yourself from becoming that person.

In all these defense strategies, as long as the world sees you as strong, confident, and faultless, they will never think to look under the rock (or behind the fig leaves) to find the real you. These strategies all prevent the small, weak, and vulnerable you from experiencing the pain of being exposed.

THE SHAME BLAME GAME

The most societally painful and damaging strategies of coping with shame are strategies of transfer. One of the most significant and frequently used is blame.

"Strategies of transfer are aroused only after some shame has begun to be felt. Such strategies of transfer aim at making someone else feel shame in order to reduce our own shame. If I feel humiliated, I can reduce that by blaming someone else, which directly transfers shame to that other person, enabling me to feel better about myself" (Kaufman 1992, 81).

After breaking my hand, it was my immediate desire to blame my eye-rolling daughter as her sister had done. I took some satisfaction from my middle daughter, TiShanté, standing up for me and placing the blame on my younger daughter till her now-epic response left us both rather speechless.

It was important for me to blame Tapricia for me breaking my hand because I didn't want to believe I had that capability in me. I didn't want to believe that I would be a person who would do such a thing and had such little control over myself. As Moore said, I had to project my badness somewhere else, so I put in on her. I am also very quick to condone the activity by saying something like, "At least I didn't hit my kid." Although there is value in not actually hitting a child, this is still an attempt to ignore the enemy within and the way it had manipulated me.

After dropping the F bombs at the congregational meeting that led to my resigning as pastor, I was less inclined to level blame on anyone. By that point, I had become more experienced with who I was and what I was doing. However, I was still able to pull off a little bit of blaming. I was able to slide in my circumstances of raising our four kids, the challenges of ministry, and overall simply trying to cope. It was a gentle sort of blaming through which I attempted to share the responsibility of my actions with some vague entity called "my circumstance." Perhaps it's why Benjamin Franklin said that we should never ruin an apology with an excuse.

Immediately after the congregation itself failed, however, I went into full-scale blame mode. I blamed the congregation, I blamed the denomination, I blamed the economy, and I may even have blamed how great we were for being persecuted like this—we were just like Jesus!! Looking back, I actually did that. Wow, that's hard to acknowledge.

I described to people how we had been so generous as to totally fund two seminarians who would later go on to plant other churches and how we had launched all of our leaders into

> *...blame leads to only one place—a very dangerous place—it leads you full circle to contempt, for yourself or for those you are attempting to blame.*

other ministries. Our (my) failure then was that we were just too generous!! Sometimes, I think I'm a genius with what I come up with to protect myself.

It was at this point, however, where I most forcefully began to blame myself and turn my anger on the only one left in my life: me.

In my experience, blame leads to only one place—a very dangerous place—it leads you full circle to contempt, for yourself or for those you are attempting to blame. Contempt is what gives rise to issues as small as locking your buddy out of school as he was trying to get in from recess to global genocidal events where an entire ethnicity is blamed for your problems. Just so we're clear on the horror blame can inflict, we have to look no further than the Holocaust. In the end, it is designed to hide your shame by elevating yourself over others.

MEMORIAL DAY—IRONIC NAME FOR A DAY I WILL NEVER FORGET

One Memorial Day weekend midway through my pastorate, I held in my arms something that absolutely did not belong there. That's all I could think about as I held the lifeless body of a 3-month-old infant boy: you do *not* belong in my arms like this.

I was in the hospital where the child was taken when he was found unresponsive at home after being put down for a nap. SIDS was the ultimate diagnosis, I believe. The family, members of my congregation, were gathered around in disbelief looking at the child. It probably surprised them when I asked if I could hold him, given my well-known propensity for being squeamish around holding newborns.

Looking back, I'm not sure why I wanted to hold him—it wasn't because I wanted to be pastoral or that I somehow wanted to do the right thing. I had already established myself for not being very pastoral with my congregation by that point anyway, so it wouldn't come as much of a surprise if I botched this, too. Bottom line, standing there, I had to (wanted to??) do whatever I could to appreciate what they were going through and that meant holding something in my arms that should have been breathing but wasn't.

I didn't *know* much when I was there, about how the baby died exactly or the mechanics around that, nor did anyone seem particularly interested in discussing them. There was just horror.

I did know there were some mechanical realities that existed in the room. There would need to be a funeral over which I would likely preside. One of the questions in the minds of everyone when something like this happens is, "Why?" It's a subtle way of attempting to find some assignable cause to the madness.

Many will blame God—an action that may forever impede a person's relationship with their God. I've heard that spouses will blame each other—one should have been watching or one should have been paying more attention. Some will try and blame God in a nice way, saying that our departed loved one was so cherished that God wanted to be closer to them and so came and got them. This approach has almost become a Christian cliché and routinely makes me ill.

During my sermon at the funeral, I remember specifically speaking out against that notion. I'm sure God could wait longer than 3 months to "call this child home," given the trauma that would ensue for the rest of us. I was convinced that God was every bit as horrified by what was happening as we were. Someday, I may find out if I was right about that or not; but for now, I believe that God never condones death, period.

Then there comes the potential for another horrible tragedy I've come to know well: self-blame.

Whenever a calf dies in my field, I blame myself. That's what shame insists I do. If it died in the weather, it was my fault for leaving it out there. If a calf gets trampled next to a hay feeder, it was my fault for not spreading out enough hay. If a calf just dies for no good reason, it's my fault for not being smart enough to have predicted the reason or—on embarrassingly frequent occasions—I have blamed myself as getting some kind of punishment from God for doing bad stuff. And these are just cows I'm talking about!! What if it were my child?

So, when I saw the mother of this child turn against herself, I knew well what she was doing, and I was powerless to stop it. The mother of this infant did blame God but she understood why God probably did it. It was to punish her for the "sin" in her life. In the end, then, she blamed herself. She believed that God took her baby from her because she, the child's mother, was "not enough" in so many ways, and God wanted her to know that He (God) was let down. I also knew there was nothing any of us were going to say or do to convince her otherwise—perhaps we shouldn't, I don't know.

I don't know how she's coped over the years. I wonder if she wakes up on Memorial Day weekend full of hurt and self-hatred for what she is still convinced is her fault, or has she found a way to absolve herself? Does she have a relationship with God, and how did that evolve over the years? Did she devolve into drinking, antidepressants, and self-hatred (the path I likely would have chosen) just attempting to make it through another day? Or has she come to a place of peace in the trauma, and does she see that although she's "not enough," she doesn't deserve to be blamed for the death of her child?

I really wish I could practice what I preach and unhook my need to transfer my shame through blame onto others or onto a self-hatred, but I get why we do it.

As someone trained in science with an extremely analytical mind, I am fully supportive of root cause analysis, as we say in corporate America. I am entirely comfortable with the idea that we need to know why a safety incident happened so we can prevent it in the future or even understand why a child has died so early or why a church had to shut its doors.

I agree wholeheartedly with the often-quoted Peter Drucker when he says, "You can't change what you don't measure." That said, blame is different. Blame does not seek to understand. Blame seeks to destroy. Blame seeks to take a rage we feel and destroy someone or something with it. Blame is something that throughout history has never actually developed into anything good, and yet we all continue to practice its seductive black magic in hope of some healing for our wounded soul or some protection against being discovered for our own inadequacies. Blame kills, and the root for our need to do it can be found in our sense of shame.

We have an insatiable need to identify a culprit—whether inside or outside ourselves, the outcome of which can be horrific. It can come in the form of lies and slander to outright suicide or genocide. So inclined are we to find a culprit as a species, that it can lead to mass cultural accep-

> *... our defense mechanisms are actually doing us more harm than good.*

tance of anything from the Holocaust to the Rwandan civil war. Robert Moore warned us that, "*The unconscious always 'keeps score.' Whenever this unconscious entity perceives an injustice or other grievance, it starts an implacable process that seeks redress, often in horrifying ways*" (Moore 2003, 199). The reason it keeps score is simple: shame requires it.

If we do nothing in this book but make people aware of the degree to which shame insists we find someone to blame and the fact that our own shame is the reason we have to assign that blame, we will have made the world a safer place for our kids.

SELF-DEFENSE BECOMES SELF-SABOTAGE

As we alluded throughout the whole book, our defense mechanisms are actually doing us more harm than good. Although they may have originally been designed to prevent us the short-term pain of feeling exposed and insufficient, they are now doing long-term, lasting damage to our ability to actually function and grow in life. In the end, our strategies will continue to alienate us from each other, our own selves, and God.

Being right has always been something of a defense strategy of mine. By being right and fighting for my rightness, I could avoid that painfully diminished sense of being "the stupid one" I mentioned earlier in this book. The problem is, no one is always right and, if they are always right, no one wants to hang out with such a person anyway!

I can remember being on the top of D Avenue hill in Cooper Township near my house. A congregational "elder" at the church I was part of was driving us to pay a hospitality visit on some congregation members; I was his "deacon" partner at the time and maybe in my mid-20s.

I can't remember what he and I were discussing, if anything, all I can remember as we poetically got to the top of that winding hill was asking myself the question, "What if Marcy (my wife) is right?"

You may now be wondering, "Right about what?" That's a good question. I don't remember. It could have been anything we were fighting about that day or week. Seriously, anything. At the same time, it doesn't matter at all.

There's a reason this moment matters in my life. Prior to that moment, I don't think I ever considered the possibility that, after or during an argument (which we had probably had that afternoon), perhaps I should shut up and just *consider* the possibility that she might be right.

At that point, I didn't know enough to ask myself the *real* questions like, *why* did I always have to be right?? Or, *what* was the internal driver behind that destructive decision? But I challenged myself to consider what might happen if I just listened to her with that question in my mind: what if she's right?

That seems simple and like something we should all be doing on a daily basis anyway. However, I wasn't doing it. More frequently, when I listened to people, I listened believing I already had all the answers and needed to show people how they were wrong. This was my way of belittling them, I guess, and, hopefully, making myself feel better about *me*.

Somehow, acknowledging my wrongness about anything from how much chlorine to add to the pool to keep back the algae to when to flush the toilet was a form of failure. Being wrong meant being stupid. (Side note: this is similar to the difference between guilt and shame. The fact I equate being wrong about something with being *stupid* is the equivalent of proclaiming myself to *be* a mistake whenever I *made* a mistake—this is how shame twists things.)

But at that moment I was describing earlier, on top of that winding hill, I challenged myself. What would happen if I assume she's right? Worse yet, what might happen if I consider the possibility that I'm wrong? My answer was telling . . . *I decided I might learn something, I might become a better person.*

Then, the more important question: Did I want to be a better person? If so, I would need to act.

The reason my answer is telling is first, it's a great example of how our defense mechanisms can start working against us. This is how self-defense can become self-sabotage. If I really want to be able to grow and become a better person (as I'm defining "better"), then my defense mechanisms were holding me back. They were repressing my ability to grow up to actually learn and become what I really wanted for myself.

The other reason my personal response is telling is because it's still all about me—the goal of learning more and becoming a better person is still very narcissistic.

It never dawned on me what would happen to my wife Marcy if I actually gave her the benefit of the doubt and listened with an intent to learn. It never dawned on me that perhaps that would affirm something in her soul that constantly felt stupid when talking to me because, according to her, I am really quite smart. Perhaps I could alleviate some of the shame-based reactions in her life by affirming what I already knew to be true about her: she was very smart and worth listening to! Shame-based defense mechanisms are both self- and other-destructive.

This, it turns out, was the case. She later admitted feeling intimidated by my intelligence and felt a need to defend herself against it because she would, through conversations with me, begin to feel small. The smaller she felt, the harder she would fight. When it comes to a fight-or-flight response, my wife fights!

Murray Stein writes of marriage as a vessel, the creation of a crucible that can help both people deal with their problems (Moore 2003, 151).

This was the crucible of being married that would start a transformation in my life. This is also why relationships matter. It's why you can't come out of shame in a vacuum. Fortunately, my wife was willing to fight because many, when they begin to feel small, choose an alternative defense strategy of becoming silenced—perhaps like they were as children. Or such people may also lash out at others even less capable of defending themselves, like children or their pets. Sadly, any response other than "fight" would have left the both of us wallowing in our shame.

> *...you can't come out of shame in a vacuum.*

However, *the main reason our defense mechanisms become self-destructive is because they prevent our personal growth and frequently aid in our personal regression. They make us become people we don't want to be and hurt our relationships with others.*

Personal growth and spiritual maturation are the professed purposes of our existence if you adhere to some of the great literature of our time spanning from the Bible to *The Road Less Traveled* by M. Scott Peck and innumerable authors in between. If we are unable to come to grips with those things preventing our spiritual growth, our ability to be ourselves and to learn, we have thwarted our basic purpose for functioning in life. If you believe your purpose in this world is anything other than this, what I have to say in this book is of little value to you, I'm afraid.

Furthermore, our defense mechanisms cut us off from each other, starving us of vital human relationships and our ability to contribute to society in general. If that goal matters to you, then your defense mechanisms can derail that goal as well.

People don't want to be around narcissists. People don't want to be around people who complain all the time. People certainly don't want to be around blamers, and many don't find a great use for being around people who are too afraid to ever speak up about anything. *This is the chief goal of shame: get us isolated so there is no chance we will become exposed and feel the pain of our "not enoughness."* Once we are isolated, we will no longer experience the potential for exposure, but we will no longer have the opportunity for growth, either.

CHAPTER 5

It's Time to Turn the Page

Somewhere in my late forties, I realized that many people loved and admired me for who I was not . . . Conversely, many loved me for who I really was, warts and all, and this was the only love that ever redeemed me (Rohr 2011, 155).

Stephen James Tollbridge is the name of a small boy who experienced life the way many small boys experience life, with full force. It was full of good stuff—stuff a small boy needs to become a healthy young man. And it was full of the bad and the ugly. There were words that told him he was a dweeb, useless, and worthy of abandon—the height of which was never really having known his biological father.

Like most children, he had little control over the things that would happen to him in life. He simply took what he was dealt as the world demanded he "grow up." Stephen James Tollbridge had some good reasons to look forward to adulthood; it seemed silly living in the pain of youth. It was time to grow up and move on. It was time to gain some control and to *become* somebody!

By age 18, Stephen James Tollbridge would cease to exist. So eager was he to discard who he was, he changed his name. Standing in his place was the man he'd always wanted to be: James Kingston. It was much better being James Kingston than Stephen James Tollbridge. James Kingston had become so competent in so many ways! He could speak—that stupid little Stephen Tollbridge couldn't even defend himself, let alone speak on behalf of anyone else.

Standing tall and assured, having left Stephen behind, James became the model adult. A capable electrician and breadwinner, he built his own house and family. He was part of the leadership team of his church. Here (in adulthood) he had strength instead of weakness, he had control instead of powerlessness, and he had courage instead of feeling fear. *This* man could change lives . . .

All was well until, over the course of several years and while attending seminary, the bible confronted James Kingston with a truth he could not avoid.

> *Matthew 18* [1] At that time the disciples came to Jesus and asked, "Who, then, is the greatest in the kingdom of heaven?" [2] He called a little child to him, and placed the child among them. [3] And he said: "Truly I tell you, unless you change and become like little children, you will never enter the kingdom of heaven.

The greatest disciple? James should at least be in the running. He was, after all, on the leadership team of one of the largest churches in town. How could they be wrong about his greatness? But Jesus grabs a child out of the crowd. A child—that's odd—they must have thought. The rabbinic classification of children placed them alongside the deaf and dumb and weak minded.

Becoming like a little child is to devolve—it's not about gaining simple trusting faith or some other endearing childish trait like cuteness or innocence. It's to become weak and vulnerable and existing to learn, experience, and transform as we live into the surprise of the kingdom of heaven.

The Bible confronts James Kingston and demands the return of Stephen James Tollbridge in all his weakness, vulnerability, and insignificance because ministry (maturity) does not flow out of strength or competence or maturity. The very word "disciple," used to describe the ones to whom the mission of Jesus was finally entrusted, is not a word of strength, but of weakness. The idea is that we are learners, which obviously implies there is something to learn—that we are lacking something. He entrusted his mission to "students," not to teachers or bishops. He entrusted his mission to those who were not enough.

Preposterous! That little grunt had nothing! He wasn't very smart—certainly not as smart as James Kingston! He had nothing to offer the world; James had so much! Stephen had no control; James was in complete control of himself and everyone else! Stephen couldn't even prevent himself from being abandoned.

It's taken us 20 or 30 years to get where we are, to gain our adulthood, and Jesus says we must recapture where we *were*, our dependence, our smallness, our vulnerability. Preposterous, but true, and *the stakes are high*: entrance into the kingdom of heaven.

It's important here again to note that I'm not attempting to propose one religion over another. I'm simply attempting to use the religion within which I have my own expertise to demonstrate how these issues of vulnerability and shame have been in existence as long as we've been keeping track of such things. I find some irony in the fact that Jesus is proposing nothing new here that key researches have not already "discovered" in their scholastic work—embrace imperfection, vulnerability, and weakness. Become your child.

I remember when I was doing an internship with an elementary school guidance counselor, I asked her what she thought it meant that we had to be like a little child to see the kingdom of heaven. Clearly, she spent her life with little children, so maybe she had some insight!

She described the way kids live life fully in the present—full force and almost defenseless to the conditions and situations around them. Children have not yet built up protective mechanisms, although many are furiously attempting to do so. She thought that vulnerability and defenselessness is what it's like "being like a child."

It's also important to make a distinction here as briefly as possible that when Jesus is referring to access to the kingdom of heaven, he's not talking about where we go when we die. He's referring to how we are alive while we are breathing. For Jesus, taking hold of whatever is small, insignificant, and weak is key to living while we are alive. Again, this argument is nothing new to many academic "shame scholars."

Shame demands the opposite of weakness and vulnerability. Shame demands we hide the weak and project the strong. Shame demands we clothe our vulnerability and add some weaponry with which to protect our being found out. Jesus suggests we actually and voluntarily expose our own vulnerability as an act of truly living life and battling against the power of shame and death in our lives.

We think that life, whether it's ministry, corporate America, or adoptive children, is intended to grow us up, but it just as much finds a child. We think the mission of life develops strengths, but it also very much causes people to embrace their weaknesses and loss. I thought that corporate America and then the Christian mission were going to make me more significant, but these things—life— just as quickly has us facing our own insignificance—all things that are at the very core of being a disciple. Facing our insignificance may be the greatest fear of a culture and a pastor struggling with their own narcissism.

The fig leaves, our defense mechanisms, have served us well. To move forward, we must lay down our weapons, as adults, to be ourselves, to welcome the vulnerabilities and imperfections. But the challenge, especially for adults, is daunting and it seems may only be attainable through the dreaded vortex of failure.

> *Most often we don't pay attention to the inner task until we have some kind of fall or failure in our outer tasks. This pattern is invariably true for reasons I have yet to fathom* (Rohr 2011, xv).

FAILURE AND THE WAY, THE TRUTH, AND THE LIFE

Failure unlocks the door to reality. I can say it no more clearly than that. If we are living in an illusion, nothing will break the illusion faster than failure.

In all the books I've read on shame, it seems to me that every author points to the importance of vulnerability as the path out. However, there are very few examples on how to actually practice whatever "vulnerability" means, and getting yourself to

> *...you have arrived at vulnerability if you are risking the opportunity to fail and to look stupid doing it.*

actually inject yourself into a situation where you are vulnerable can be a *great* challenge. I suggest you will know *you have arrived at vulnerability if you are risking the opportunity to fail and to look stupid doing it.*

Some have suggested that we can't really practice vulnerability, that being vulnerable is simply what it means to be human. All we can do is accept the condition and live into it rather than putting so much energy into avoiding this unavoidable reality. If that's the case, the way to vulnerability lies with putting down the defenses and preparing for failure, as it will find us all soon enough.

Failure is the great equalizer. *Failure is a forced awakening to your smallness,* if we choose to use it as such. In fact, the reason it's so powerful is that a "failure event" is typically one that dresses you up to parade around among your peers in your finest outfit only to find out you've shown up completely naked—naked in your bankruptcy or demotion, naked in your addiction or financial incompetence. So, if vulnerability is truly the way out, and failure is abject vulnerability, failure is the way out. It actually reminds me why Jesus declared himself as "the way," yet was poetically crowned "king" as a mockery as he hung naked on the cross.

> *Failure is a forced awakening to your smallness ...*

Let's pause right here to acknowledge something. We all know this. You can go on Google right now. In fact, do that. Go on Google right now and search, "you must fail to succeed," and look at the absolute barrage of quotes and examples you get on this subject—from famous and powerfully successful people.

Even some corporations propose to thrive on it. 3M Company is one that comes to mind, as does Elon Musk: "Failure is an option here. If things are not failing, you are not innovating enough" (Reingold 2005).

In fact, you might have one such quote framed on your desk as we speak! Every single person you admire has failed brutally before being the success you see in front of you. Yet, we avoid failure as if it will lead to death.

The fact that we fear failure is the most illogical proposition in the cosmos. The one thing everyone consistently tells us—people we admire, trust, and hope to be like—is that victory comes *only* through failure. *Logically, we should be lining up at the failure banquet to get a heaping portion instead of running for the exits* and declaring it not an option for our lives.

Failure is the one thing we rail against—at least if people are going to find out about it. Failing is the most horrible of enemies. If you don't believe me, ask your pastor what their worst fear is. Ask your

CEO what her or his worst fear is. Ask your parents what their worst fear was as parents, and then ask yourself what one thing you will avoid at all cost! Our fear is so great, many of us won't even *try* to succeed.

This, my friends, if nothing else, will tell you about the horrible power of shame. We know in our heads that our "imperfections are a gift" and that "failure is the road to success," yet we fear those very things that we know will bring us where we want to be. The illogic of that tells us there is a hidden motivator inside us that is working *against* our spiritual maturation and *against* our ultimate victory and success all in the name of protecting us from the potential of pain and humiliation—the pain of being exposed in our weaknesses and imperfections.

* * *

Marcy was just 31 years old when she got the call. She had been a teacher only 6 short years, but the administration in her school district had seen her capabilities and the deep caring she had for those kids. They wanted her to take the job as principal of the school where she was teaching.

As you probably know from my own story, I would have jumped at the chance at that time in my life. My ego and the need to be affirmed would have manipulated me into doing anything where I thought I could get more power and more accolades and continue to preserve the image I wanted to project to people. Those were not Marcy's concerns. She would very much prefer to run from the spotlight with everything she has.

Regarding this job in particular, she was concerned she was "not enough" to do well. She wasn't old enough. She wasn't experienced enough. She wasn't smart enough. She wasn't gifted enough. She had limitations but seemed to think she was the only one with them. She knew she was a good teacher, a *great* teacher. But she was afraid of the new job even though her passion was to make education a powerful thing for the entire school—a passion her administration clearly saw.

The primary battle with shame has to do with overcoming the horror in discovering we're limited and then deciding what to do with that information. We are limited. Everyone is. That's the news flash. It's time to move on.

Fortunately, the administration saw through her fear of failure. Fortunately for those hundreds even thousands of children who have gone through her program, she overcame her fear to try. Many of us won't. Today, having failed miserably at being a pastor, I'm not sure I would try today either even though a spot in my soul thinks I need to in order to vindicate my past failures!

> *The primary battle with shame has to do with overcoming the horror in discovering we're limited and then deciding what to do with that information.*

Sadly, this is the horrible power of your inner critic who was once necessary in preventing you from experiencing the brutal pain of exposure to the world. This demonstrates the power of your inner critic to derail your life in that it is now preventing your very maturation into a complete human being. This is *your* life, not the life of your inner critic. You are now an adult, and it's time to discharge this loyal soldier and live your own life—certainly to fail—but to become who you've always really been.

Shame is the bus taking us where we don't want to go using our fear of pain to chart the course.

Ironically, though, there's a great deal of argument that suggests there is a hidden war in your subconscious that may actually bring about failure in hopes of saving you from yourself. I spoke recently with a young man who has been sabotaging his relationship with his wife, certain that she will one day leave him anyway. My oldest daughter has asked me why she sabotages her relationships, although you don't have to pry very far into her history to see the trail of abandonment she is expecting to continue in her life.

One of the refrains we traditionally made when raising our kids was, "How did they not know they were going to get caught?" Such was the case one day when our son Troy was out with the car. We only had two rules with the car: we need to know where you are and who you're with. On this particular day, he avoided both of those rules and, when he was supposed to be at work, he drove by our house with his friends. There were 800 ways to get where he was going that didn't involve driving right past our house. He's not stupid. How could he not know he was going to get caught?

The same question came to mind when General David Petraeus—leader of the Central Intelligence Agency—was busted embroiled in an affair with his biographer. How did he get caught? Emails. Hello? How does the leader of the CIA not know how to delete emails? Jimmy Swaggart and Hugh Grant out shopping on public streets for prostitutes. How can they not know they will get caught? Tiger Woods?

Teenage boy out for a drive with his friends or leader of the CIA, when our subconscious believes we are a fraud, and we are in need of some life-saving vulnerability as psychologists suggest, we will set ourselves up for vulnerability at sometimes a horrific level. It's as if we can finally get caught in order to come clean with the world about the fact that we are imperfect.

It's the hope of our subconscious to set our soul free from attempts at perfection to be just plain human.

This may have been what I was up to when I went to start a church . . .

THE SET UP FOR THE FALL

I probably should have seen it coming. I had set myself up for a colossal failure. The secretive motive behind all my decisions had set itself up for quite a quagmire. I needed to do something "great" in order to prevent feeling any pain from being "insignificant," and I was willing to go to great lengths—with the help of shame—to pursue said greatness in hopes of cloaking my weakness.

The dilemma is/was that when we have allowed our shame to set ourselves up in a position of greatness, we are also at risk of a more horrific fall. Shame knows that once we have achieved the greatness we thought we needed, it will drive us all the harder to get to the next level. I'm not sure when the phrase "the next level" evolved, but it's thoroughly embedded in our drive systems now. Those of us with high shame drives are always attempting to get to the next level.

During my interview to be allowed to start planting new churches for our denomination, it was important for me to demonstrate the strength of my past behavior because, as they said, it is a great predictor of future success.

I can specifically remember the meeting—the plush blue velvet chairs in the church committee meeting room (why do churches all have the same weird chairs that no one would have in their house??). There was a group of people each wearing their own fig leaves, and they were there to assess me. It was important for them to let me know how hard it was being a pastor and that it wasn't something that should be entered into lightly.

Little did I know at the time this was their shame talking. It's important for all of us to project how difficult our work is so that others will hold us in higher regard. In my brief experience of life, the two most difficult jobs I've experienced are roofing and dairy farming. Those people have hard jobs. Pastors get sabbaticals—they get time off—3 to 6 months at a crack—to rest, reflect, and grow. It's a great tradition, but not something the rest of the world gets to experience, that's for sure!! Imagine you roofers out there getting 6 months paid leave every 3 or 4 years!

Ironically, when I became a pastor, I was riddled with shame in telling people that's what I did for a living. I was riddled with shame and would always have to defend myself (which, as you recall, was my shame strategy of defense) and explain to people what I did all day. It's one reason going back would be difficult. As a part of corporate America, it feels like I can actually tell people I am being a productive member of society. I'm not saying all pastors feel that way, but I sure did.

Anyway, the first thing I did when challenged was dismiss the difficulty of their jobs by pronouncing without hesitation that it was *nothing* compared to what I had been doing. This likely generated even more feelings of shame in them and caused them to dig in even deeper against me, even though they were really defending themselves. But what I remember specifically are the exact words that came out of my mouth at that moment. I said, "I have never failed at anything."

It didn't seem like bragging when I said it, even though I'm sure that's how it was perceived. Ironically, it's what they were hoping to see and it was all mechanically quite true.

- **I had graduated from an engineering program with honors in 4 ½ years that usually takes 5.**
- **I had all my tuition paid for—twice—through academic scholarships.**
- **I used the money to buy a house while in college, and I rented rooms out to my friends.**
- **I became the youngest business development manager in my company and the first one to ever be allowed to do the job from home.**
- **I had successfully launched a cattle operation with no background in farming.**
- **I had graduated with honors from seminary in the same length of time it took my peers, while I was working full time.**
- **My program at my home church took Sunday evening worship from about 50 to 300 to 700 people.**
- **And, let's not forget, I had done all this after being an atheist a short time before!**

Looking at the list printed up like that, I'm reminded that I actually was pretty "accomplished." But, there was a problem . . . The problem was a problem of motives. The problem was a problem of the soul. The problem was I was attempting to lead in a faith that says the first shall be last, and the last shall be first, and the greatest are the least. The problem was I needed to live into the message myself in order to effectively lead others there. Past accomplishments didn't translate into being a successful pastor. I also learned that pastoring was actually more about transformation than productivity if you do it sincerely. I wasn't ready for that.

On my way to redemption, one thing (at least) still stood in my path: failure. To find my way to this place, I would have to find my meaning, purpose, and hope in the midst of failure—the collapse of my valuation system, the failure of my false self. Success was not an option if I were going to succeed.

> *You will and must "lose" at something. This is the only way that Life-Fate-God-Grace-Mystery can get you to change, let go of your egocentric preoccupations, and go on the further and larger journey* (Rohr 2011, 66/67).

The problem? "A win doesn't feel as good as a loss feels bad, and the good feeling doesn't last as long as the bad. Not even close" (Agassi 2009, 165).

As I was getting ready to launch our new church, I can still remember sitting around the conference table with the chairman of the oversight board of the congregation, the lead pastor of the church, and a few other committee chairs. We were discussing how the new church plant would go and how it fit into the congregation I was part of at the time—their congregation.

> *"A win doesn't feel as good as a loss feels bad ..."*

As we sat around the table, the committee chair for outreach at the church, a vice president at a very successful corporate medical operation, tried to help me understand what was at stake with the planning process.

He said to me: *Failure is not an option.*

I understand where the idea that "failure is not an option" comes from in *corporate America*. It is rather dramatic and helps us think we are landing on the moon, which is what has made it part of the bread and butter of corporate American folklore and reality. Failure leads to dismissal. Period. Failure leads to loss. Period. What I'm surprised about is the use of this statement in the areas of the church, particularly when the church itself was founded upon failure much more than success.

I never forgot that moment. On one hand, I was scared to death of failure because it would mean I was a failure (remember that's how shame talks). *In my heart,* I knew I had to do everything to prevent failure—not so we wouldn't waste our resources but so that I wouldn't look bad. On the other hand, *I knew in my head* that failure absolutely was an option. I knew this for two reasons:

1. Along with the thinking of Elon Musk, I knew that innovation only comes through failure. In fact, one of my most favorite quotes at the time was "*if you're not falling, you're not skiing hard enough.*" If the church was going to innovate, it would have to risk failure.
2. The entire Christian mission was given to people who had repeatedly failed their mentor.

FAILURE, A BIBLICAL REALITY

My seminary experience championed the idea of the church as a community of people "on mission" . . . that always adds some flash and glamour. Who wouldn't want to be "on mission" for God? With the theme song of *Mission Impossible* pounding in the background, the image of Tom Cruise scaling the face of a sheer rock mountain with nothing but his bare hands comes to mind. As he reaches the peak, he gets his mission, an impossible mission. Only you know that no mission would be impossible if you recruited talent like that.

As I previously discussed, it's said that past behavior is a predictor of future success. When I became a new church start pastor, I went through all kinds of tests to demonstrate I had shown myself capable in the past of doing similar things.

For example, my experience in corporate America demonstrated my ability to start up new businesses and effectively lead a team toward a particular vision. If you have proven yourself capable of scaling unscalable rock cliffs, trusting yourself in almost blind leaps, hanging precariously by your fingertips, odds are, no mission is probably really impossible and failure need not even be considered an option. You always know how a Tom Cruise movie will end.

If only the average disciple were so competent. If only the average human were so competent. If only *any* human were so competent and without faults or failings. Here is the irony with the church: the church is the one organization that professes to *know* this and *embrace* it while we attempt to live this double life of invincible warriors in the kingdom of God.

We think that the "heart of God" that pulled us into this life of service to the word of God and his people will be our unfailing ally, but it turns out that few fields of work expose the ego so relentlessly to the ruses of vanity and pride (Peterson 1992, 85).

In fact, at one point, [23] Jesus turned and said to Peter, "Get behind me, Satan! You are a stumbling block to me; you do not have in mind the concerns of God, but merely human concerns" (*Matthew 16*).

Satan?! Peter's "the Rock"! How does Jesus intend to build his church upon Satan?! How did Peter get from "the rock" to the "stumbling block" in the exact same conversation? How did he go from the foundation of all the Son of God would be doing in the world to the antichrist in five little verses?

The word "stumbling block" that Jesus uses to confront Peter is actually the Greek word *scandalon* from which we get our word "scandal." It's funny how closely linked the words "scandal" and "church" are in our world and in the Bible itself. We are even shocked when the church finds itself in another scandal as if the church is suddenly full of mission impossible–caliber people instead of regular old disciples like you and me, prone to mistakes and failure.

Here's the worst fear of a Christian: having Jesus look into your soul and say, "What the hell are you doing? Do you have any idea who I am? Do you think I *need* your protection? Do you think you're helping me? Not only are you not helping me, but you are a stumbling block to me. Not only are you not helping me, but you are preventing me from doing what I need to do!"

Limitations and imperfections are the heart of what it means to be human, but we dread the day when we come face to face with ours, especially when we find that they are hurting the cause we care about the most. It's why my wife didn't want to take the principal position. It's why many of us never move. We know we are human, and we don't want to let anyone down.

I would wake up some mornings scared out of my mind that I was not helping but hurting the cause of Christ in my inability to acknowledge him. I would wake up scared out of my mind that I had no idea what I was doing as a minister and that I may very well be leading people onto a path in direct opposition to the Son of God—no, that I *was*, at times, leading people on such a path. Some mornings, I would wake up and hear a voice in my head saying, "What the hell are you doing?! Do you actually think you're helping me?" Maybe roofing would have been easier . . .

> *Limitations and imperfections are the heart of what it means to be human...*

This, it seems is the life of the disciple: a constant tension between worship and doubt, belief and unbelief, knowledge and ignorance, heaven and hell, and, like it or not, success and failure. The life of the church has forever stood in the tension between declaring Jesus to be the Christ, and standing defiantly *between* him and his mission. This is the church; this is discipleship; this is the nature of the people Christ has chosen to represent him.

So *why?* Why build the church on something so remarkably inconsistent and inadequate? Why build the church on the very thing that will be the stumbling block? Why would you build your church on the thing that only has its own interest in mind and not the interests of God, the one it's supposed to be serving?

Perhaps because the mission of God is not to protect Himself from scandal or even to build a church, but to give people life and the path for that project leads through failure. As such, I can only conclude that building this church on this trembling foundation will land us where it left Peter: weeping bitterly at our inabilities, our limitations, our "not enoughness," as part of our own journey toward life whether we like it or not.

FREEDOM ONLY THROUGH FAILURE

I'm pretty sure my daughters all believe I am some version of the greatest person they have ever known; one of my girls may actually be preparing a monument to honor me after my death. I'm pretty sure there is no better feeling in the world than knowing your children think that way about you.

We get to where we put people on pedestals or we demonize them—I think that too is something our own shame has a hand in doing. Neither reality is probably true or entirely deserved, but we have a seeming necessity to do it. To some extent, I wonder if psychologists would call these *transference relationships* where we are transferring our own need for self-hatred or exceptionalism onto someone else that may be necessary for our survival as humans. The Bible is no exception.

We have made Peter our hero and Judas our villain. When, in reality, they both failed Jesus horribly, and they were both left with a bitter awareness of their "not enoughness." Perhaps, in that regard, they both met Jesus' goals for them.

The Bible portrays the original disciples as human—sometimes, they are worse than others but always imperfect. The worst two moments ever recorded occurred back to back—Peter's failure and then Judas'—argu-

> *We get to where we put people on pedestals or we demonize them—I think that too is something our own shame has a hand in doing.*

ably the two most famous of them. Both failed at critical points in their allegiance to their leader, the one they most wanted to impress. In the end, they all deserted him.

Now, if past behavior is a predictor of future success, you don't give folks like this much of a mission. Yet, here they are (shy Judas) on the mountain with the Son of God. What if Judas had not killed himself? Would he be standing among them on the mountain getting instructions along with Peter? I wonder if Peter considered suicide over seeing Jesus again after what he had done, the same way Judas took his own life. Perhaps he remembered what Jesus had said when they were first sent out in mission back in Chapter 10 . . .

Matthew 10 [33] But whoever disowns me before others, I will disown before my Father in heaven.

. . . and wondered if it would be better to simply call it a day . . . a week . . . a life. What sort of a mission can you launch on the backs of such men?

It's been argued that such folks were chosen, so it would be clear Jesus accepted all types of losers to his mission. This reasoning reminds me of AYSO's motto: everyone plays. And, it's great being inclusive and all, but since the salvation of the world is at stake, you'd think such a mission would at least want to access the top third of the population. Leading to option #2: The mission was not the responsibility of humans, but of God. This reasoning sounds great, but then why include humans at all? Both arguments may very well be true in part, but possibly incomplete.

I wonder if the mission of God is intended, at least in part, to land humans at this place with Peter and Judas: weeping bitterly at their inability to follow Christ in mission. Human beings weeping bitterly at the way they've fallen short of what their savior has asked . . . simply to be acknowledged. Human beings weeping bitterly at the way doubt has overtaken worship despite their best attempts at worship and belief. Is it possible that arriving at this place of weeping bitterly is actually the mission of God? Is this the point of human salvation?

I wonder if Judas made it into heaven. I wonder if, at the very end, he was able to grab hold of enough of who Jesus was to "qualify" . . . or did he simply go too far? What about Peter? Did he ever repent or did he just weep bitterly? Did he spend the rest of his ministry on earth desperately trying to earn back that horrible night? Did he spend the remainder of his life launching churches to assuage his shame and not enoughness?

Matthew never answers; he's remarkably and painfully silent. He never tells us not to worry, that everyone was fine, but leaves us with no answers. Or maybe, just maybe, who gets in and out of heaven wasn't the overriding concern of Matthew, unlike modern Christianity. Maybe Matthew's overriding concern was to show us "the way, the truth, and the life" comes through failure and uncertainty. Regardless, Matthew leaves us only with a desperate hope in the ultimate forgiving, reconciling, healing, redeeming grace of God in Christ despite the most horrible acts of abandonment that are heaped upon him. Matthew just leaves us with a picture of being called to mission *despite* our past behavior.

For the shame-based person, the battle between winning and preventing losing will forever be a principal, driving force in projecting an image to the world that is different from how you might perceive yourself. This is true whether you are in ministry, on a farm, in corporate America, or a stay-at-home parent.

CORPORATE EXECUTIVE BECOMES CHURCH PASTOR

One depiction of the new corporate executive I came across in my doctoral research on narcissism helped me understand how I was approaching my pastoral functions as well. I don't believe this was the author's goal with his book, but it helped me see the similarities between shame-based individuals in ministry and corporate America.

> *[A] person who seeks to experience . . . 'the exhilaration of running his team and gaining victories.' He wants to 'be known as a winner, and his deepest fear is to be labeled a loser' . . . in all his personal relations, the gamesman depends on the admiration or fear he inspires in others to certify his credentials as 'winner'* (Lasch 1991, 44/45) . . . *He advances through corporate ranks not by serving the organization but by convincing his associates that he possesses the attributes of a 'winner'* (Lasch 1991, 61).

During the rush of the first couple years of launching a congregation, I could always hear the wondering voice in my head when I was approached with a new relationship in the congregation: "What can you do for me?" or "What can you add to us?" Any relationships I was forming were always in danger of becoming instrumental—people were always in danger of becoming my tools to meet my own objectives.

The whole process *as I experienced it* is set up such that the "young executive" can experience the exhilaration of running a team to victory and is built largely on the admiration or fear the executive is able to engender in the launch team.

In the beginning, while the process is task oriented and measurable, the fear of failure and disappointment was certain to drive me to succeed at all costs in very much the same way I felt in corporate America. The question before me always seemed to be, "How will I rally and structure a people to grow the kingdom of God?"

Fear of not meeting the projections was always overwhelming to me, whether in corporate America or in new church development, as it quickly translates into yet another revelation of the personal shame each of us narcissistically wounded pastors carries.

> *Falling short would show the world that I, quite simply, had failed and, more relevantly, was a failure.*

Falling short would show the world that I, quite simply, had failed and, more relevantly, *was* a failure. Protecting my impotence from being on display for the world was a primary concern, even though we worship a savior who died impotent. This fear was then transferred to our fledgling congregation; it was manipulated by the unspoken threat of withholding nourishing pieces of approval, whipping the early launch team into a mad push of productivity.

Eugene Peterson gave me an early warning from his own experiences in ministry in a book that became pivotal in my ministry:

> *It is a prevalent attitude of pastors toward congregations [to see them not as a resource to be cared for but as loot] and one that I have held more often than I like to admit. When I take up that attitude, I see the congregation as raw material to manufacture into an evangelism program, or mission outreach, or a Christian Education learning center. Before I know it, I'm pushing and pulling, cajoling and seducing, persuading and selling* (Peterson 1992, 132).

I woke up to this reality one evening after worship rehearsal. I stood in the parking lot of our worship building with one of our worship leaders. She was describing to me how frazzled she was from attempting to put her sermon together for the following week. Because of her own narcissistic wounding, she's the new church start member every pastor hopes comes their way from the beginning: effective, gifted, productive, easily motivated by shame and fear, and willing to help out in any way for a little affirmation from the right person.

I've become aware that these manipulative drives are a fundamental part of my own narcissistic personality in my home, the church, and in corporate America.

> *The manipulator perceives that another's goals conflict with his own, he intends to influence the other person and employs deception in the influencing process . . . This is a conscious, not unconscious, process . . . is carefully planned and executed, often by first eliciting the other person's trust and then exploiting this trust* (Capps 1993, 23).

Suddenly, I realized I had become the pastor I never wanted to be. Here was a wonderfully talented human being who was working for everything she was worth in order to help me build this monument not to her, or even her God, but to me. My monument needed female preachers, a powerful worship service, pastors for impact congregations, and something for the kids to do while the adults were doing "important" stuff. She was willing to do it all, if I just reminded her she was great.

The next day, I sat in my office (a booth at the local Burger King), in shock and horror at what I'd become (shame). This is where "error" turns to "self-hatred" for the shame-based person. As humans, we make mistakes, but that does not make us a mistake. I'm sure it is a place many pastors frequently find themselves—yet still more afraid to fail than to stop manipulating and run the risk of failure.

In the end, it failed. It no longer exists. The reasons are numerous and multifaceted, but it exposed me to the way, the truth, and the life. **The truth** was, **I was not enough.** This failure and realization probably should have caused me to pause to work through those issues. Instead, the symptoms of my shame disease kicked into high gear—particularly blame.

There is one great obstacle presenting itself to us on our journey to and through failure: Fear.

CHAPTER 6

Fear Not

The only thing we have to fear is fear itself.
— F. D. Roosevelt, 1932

It was the summer of 2010, and I was at a cottage bonfire with the extended family on Torch Lake in Northern Michigan at the sandbar made famous by Kid Rock. My nephew had graduated high school, and his mother (my sister) suggested we go around the campfire and give my nephew some tips for moving into his next phase of life.

As usual, I wasn't listening to the others (a shortcoming of mine) because I was busy wondering what I would offer when my turn came. My turn arrived, and I leaned into the campfire for effect and said, "Fear not."

It sort of made the group pause for a moment wondering, I think, what kind of advice that was. It certainly wasn't something straight-forward like "get through college" or "don't go in debt." In the pause that followed, sensing a need for explanation, I asked the group if they knew the most frequent command in the Bible. They offered a series of "thou shalt nots," until I said, "The most frequent command in the Bible is 'fear not.'"

> *"Sometimes," he said, "we even fail to make a decision at all because we are afraid."*

I followed that up with another question: "Do you know *why* that might be the most frequent command in the Bible?" Again, there was silence. I offered this explanation: "Because the majority of humanity's stupid decisions—decisions they would later regret—are decisions made in fear. When you make a decision because you are afraid of 'this happening' or 'that repercussion,' you are likely making a poor decision."

My brother, my junior in years but my senior in the escapades of corporate America (becoming CEO of a $3.5 billion publically traded company at age 40ish), pointed at me and said, "He's exactly right. In our company, we would make such better decisions if we simply weren't afraid of making the wrong decision or what would happen to us if we made the right decision. Sometimes," he said, "we even fail to make a decision at all because we are afraid."

It was a moment around the campfire to be sure—a moment of sincere contemplation and reflection. The moment was quickly broken as my brother, returning to his junior status in years, put the flashlight under his chin so as to light his face like they do in horror movies and declared ominously for the rest of the evening "fear not" in his best possible Darth Vader voice.

I told my brother we needed to write an entire book on the dangers of fear in decision making that would sort of be a partner to this book on shame. I know from ministry that the greatest fear among pastors is the fear of failure, and I believe based on research and my own time in corporate America that the greatest fear among entrepreneurs and CEOs is the same. I know that my brother has been working at reducing the levels of fear in his own organization as a pillar to the culture he's attempting to develop there, so I called him to discuss coauthoring something specific to corporate America.

He was intrigued but was rushing off to meet with his board, as they were close to announcing their quarterly results to investors. As we were concluding the call, he said, almost to himself, "I'm not sure I'm the right guy for this—we certainly haven't seen the results from my efforts." I hung up and tended to agree with him. How could you tell the story of the value of reducing fear-based decisions in a corporate environment (secular or religious) with no proof it actually worked? Perhaps the tides would turn at his company, and we could announce to the world we (he) had the winning formula!

On October 26, 2016—a couple weeks after my first conversation with my brother—they announced quarterly earnings that beat most Wall Street expectations, and the stock dropped 6 percent. I don't know what that feels like. I don't know what it's like being paid that kind of money, having that many bosses (investors), and letting them all down. I don't know what it's like in that context or the voices that now must be in your head attempting to convince you to either stay the course or abandon ship—voices saying "You can do this" and "What the hell are you doing?" at the same time.

I do recall the previous quarter when they beat Wall Street expectations, and the stock rose 12 percent. I texted my congratulations, and he replied saying, "It's good to finally see your efforts paying off." But today, those same efforts had not impressed anyone. Here he was, a new, young CEO with grand ideas on how a company should be run, and watching as the company devalued quarter after quarter. What does a person feel like in that situation?

While I don't know what *that's* like, I do recall watching my own congregation dwindle into nonexistence—the congregation that my denomination had entrusted me to launch based on my vision for the church. They entrusted me with their name, their money, and their reputation and my vision—the way I thought church should be run. It failed. The problem was, I felt like *I* was a failure. It didn't bother me as much that I had failed or that my ideas had failed, but that it was now evident to everyone who believed in me that *I* was a failure—they were, after all, *my* ideas and it was *my* vision. That, if you recall, is shame talking. I had been exposed for who I really was, ignorant in the areas of pastoring now adding my name to the "walk of shame."

But this day, October 26, was different. I texted my brother and said, "*Now* is the time." I told him that I had originally agreed with him that it would be better if his company was succeeding because it would prove him (us) right in our theory that reducing fear improves the chance of success. However, I think that it's actually now that this message matters because it's now that he may have to practice what he preaches. It's now, down 6 percent on earnings that beat expectations but didn't impress, that fear will most likely be knocking on his door suggesting he make decisions he may believe in his heart are not the right decisions for the company, their employees, or their shareholders. I told him, "Now is the time when you must practice what you preach and 'fear not' little brother. Fear not."

ANTHONY

Anthony is a young sales manager in a global industrial company whose goal is to be CEO as well. He describes the thrill he gets from being goal oriented—whether it's the sales targets he has for his team, his personal fitness objectives, or his corporate strivings.

I asked why it was so important to him—why did it matter to him personally? He said he wanted to be a contributor to his company. He wanted to see himself and his organization being successful. All things admirable in our society, as perhaps they should be. "But why?" I pressed. What does that do for you, personally? His answer was quick and direct, as if rehearsed, "Because I don't want to be a lazy, f-ing turd."

Ironically, this attack was not geared at people who had different objectives than he had for himself; I don't think he would call someone not driven to be CEO a "lazy, f-ing turd." In fact, when asked which one of the two of us would be more likely to be CEO, he said he would, but never implied I was a lazy turd. It was a name he seemed to save for himself.

In the end, this is our world, and these are the names we call ourselves. *These are the names that, though we hide them back somewhere deep in our psyche, they continue to call to us from the gallows of our soul.* These are the names we hear that attempt to dictate our actions and decisions in our attempts to prevent becoming that thing we fear most—that name we have for ourselves may actually be true of us.

I suggested to him that perhaps his primary motivation for all he was doing was not the enjoyment of the doing itself but rather the fear of what *not* doing it represented. As long as he was accomplishing his goals, he could obtain the sense of relief that comes with a demonstration that he was no lazy, f-ing turd.

I asked him as I asked those around the campfire if he knew what the most frequent command in the Bible was. He listed off things associated with the Ten Commandments and anything beginning with "do this" or "don't do that." He listed off anything and everything that could be used against him if anyone wanted to prove in a court of law that he was a loser and incompetent. He was shocked when I told him that the most frequent command was "Fear not." Yet, his primary motives for his actions seem to be driven by fear— fear that he might become what he secretly despised.

Fear frequently catapults us into making the wrong decisions and pursuing the wrong actions in the name of self-preservation, or it causes us to succumb to a rather catatonic state of inaction. It's hard, after all, to do something wrong or stupid when you do nothing at all.

Interestingly, CEO types are frequently plagued with the exact same personality. Pursuing their goals for fear of _____ [fill in the blank]. There is a great fear of failure in that community, as there is in the pastorate. Anthony expressed the same fear. Of most importance here is not that the fear of failure exists, but what the real fear is: the fear of having been discovered for who you're afraid you just might be—a "lazy, f-ing turd." Although the type, Anthony included, is thrilled by the idea of risking failure, at least until they have failed at least once.

Yet, we hang signs with pithy sayings on our office walls to remind us to adventure regardless of the potential for failure. We sing songs and read books, all of which encourage us to live life fully (my personal favorite is *Dead Poet's Society*). We look at successful people and recount the times they failed, never mentioning those who just simply continued to fail in their adventures and never really win anything. My mother bought me a shirt that said, "Not all who wander are lost." If she was referring to me, she must have confused my lostness with some valuable form of contribution to society (wandering) because I actually was lost!!

> *In the end, it's the fear of being exposed. It's the fear that people will see us for who we really are. It's shame.*

Oddly, fear grips almost every facet of our existence, from cradle to grave. Fear of being forgotten, fear of being remembered. Fear of failure—my personal favorite—which of course, is really a result of fear of looking stupid, or maybe fear of being discovered for actually being stupid! Fear of dying. Fear of living. Fear of speaking and fear of not being heard. In the end, it's the fear of being exposed. It's the fear that people will see us for who we really are. It's shame. And it's hiding in each of us to one degree or another, and it's causing us to be manipulated into making decisions we otherwise wouldn't have wanted to.

The question we all face, going back to Chapter 1, is "Why?" Why do we do what we do? If the answer boils back down to fear, then shame is motivating and manipulating your decisions.

The by-products of shame – fear, blame, and disconnection (Brown 2008, xiv).

Fear is more of a tool shame uses to get what it wants. Remember, for me, shame is a fear of being exposed as "not enough." Shame is a fear of being found out that you are weak, small, fat, stupid, whatever else you want to add or all of the above.

It's in and through fear that shame manipulates us to make the decisions we otherwise would not choose to make. Fear is how the snake got Eve to take the apple and fear is how shame is getting us to do things and leave things undone.

One way I've considered overcoming that issue is to challenge people to have a better understanding of themselves—to consider that they know more than they think they do. I tried this approach frequently with my mother-in-law who would rarely speak at church meetings because she didn't want to

> *There will come a day when you have to accept that you are weak and someone else is stronger. It's here that, with my brother, flashlight under my chin, I say in a bold voice, "FEAR NOT."*

say something stupid, even though when she did speak it was never stupid and almost always helpful. The problem with that approach alone is that, right now, if my mother-in-law read this, she would probably think "*almost* always helpful??" When was it not?? She would forget the fact that almost every single time she spoke it was helpful, in a mad hunt for that *one* time when it wasn't.

Along with trying to convince people (myself included) that we are more than we think we are (which is a noble cause), we must also and maybe first acknowledge that there will come a day when you're wrong, and everyone may find out about it. There may come a day when you venture and lose, and the world will know. There will come a day when you have to accept that you are weak and someone else is stronger. It's here that, with my brother, flashlight under my chin, I say in a bold voice, "FEAR NOT." This too is part of being human. This too is something we all share in common, even though you think you may be the only one.

YOU CAN'T MISS WHAT YOU DON'T MEASURE

We are taught to view achievement as the measure of our intrinsic worth or adequacy. We are further taught to strive after success and to measure it directly through our accomplishments. Hence, external performance becomes the measure of self-esteem. Striving for success can breed anxiety in the form of fear of failure because success is never entirely within our control (Kaufman 1992, 32).

A small group of explorers huddled in a church lounge once a week in late 1999. Full of hubris and world-changing hopes, we would have to decide how we would define this voyage we were about to undertake. We would talk of mission statements and vision in every sense corporate America had taught us to think of such things. By some connection of words, I was able to paint a picture of the Northwest Passage—the church, in its grand utopia—that caught the attention of this group, even though I had never been there myself. I remember being shocked that such a group would be willing to risk life and limb to undertake a voyage even their captain hadn't yet traveled. However, we would finally lead North America into what it meant to "do church right."

The question we failed to ask ourselves in that moment, the question

I've come to believe is the root question of all actions, the question I grilled my daughter with that we failed to consider was "Why?" Why did we need to do that? Why was that so important to us?

We likely would have provided answers like: we want to be holy, we want to be great for God, we want to be meaningful. All these answers go back to the garden, as we hear the snake remind us that "we are not enough" and that we should strive to be like God himself. Remember that even Jesus, the person we purposed to be following, could not bring about the church on earth.

Be that as it may, we needed to succeed.

How would we know we'd been successful? Would it be the presence of a building where there previously was none? Would it be new "converts" to the faith? How many? Better, we decided, we'd measure success not by the number of converts, but by the extent of our own conversion.

We decided we wanted to be a people who loved God and loved our neighbor—something we all agreed we presently were not doing. To live into this vision, we would certainly have to walk *his* path and experience *his* experiences. In short, we would have to be transformed into *his* image. If we attempted to live into this vision, we would certainly arrive at our goal. It sounded too romantic to possibly fail.

Anyone with any experience in vision statements knows this one leaves a great deal to be desired. It lacks a number of key requirements of any vision statement I had previously developed for either ministry or business. For starters, just like the rest of our criteria for success, it's not particularly measurable (my previous congregation had a mission of reaching 1% of the 137,500 unchurched people in their neighborhood). Second, there's nothing in it that has any sense of timeline, and it would be nearly impossible to determine if we'd ever arrived or if this destination was even "arrivable."

I wonder if Lewis and Clarke had a vision statement. If they did, it would probably have said something like, "Find the Northwest

Passage before winter." It would be measurable and have a timeline. It could easily be sold to management and funding institutions. However, it would have missed the real work they would ultimately accomplish as they saw things they wouldn't have seen and experienced things they wouldn't have experienced had they not headed out on the voyage. These must have been the things truly motivating them—the love of experience. How fundable is an expedition of people who simply "want to experience a bunch of stuff"? How long will a sales manager or CEO get by without numeric success? They won't.

Was the goal excessively narcissistic (in that it was all about us)? Perhaps. Perhaps not. Was our goal measurable? No. But 16 people sat in a room and decided we'd know we were successful if somehow we were more like Christ tomorrow than we were today. It made us feel something like Ethan Hunt (*Mission Impossible*) hanging from those cliffs on a mission for God. It felt good and brave and right. Little did we know what we were in for; little did we know that the image of Christ is not one of grandiosity, success, or heroics but one of smallness, meekness, and humility.

On the surface, we failed to be either Catholic or evangelical—a point captured in the one and only article done about our ministry by the local newspaper. We weren't openly compelled to make other people buy into our vision of what it meant to be a human being or what it meant to be a Christian. It's what *we* claimed was of utmost importance to us, to experience the ride, regardless of where we ended up. It felt holy to not be "results" oriented for a change. It felt right, perhaps naïve, but right.

However, I quickly realized that just because you're wearing boots, you haven't shaved in a week, and you smell like crap, doesn't mean you're a cowboy. I was no cowboy. I wanted results regardless of what I said. In the end, it was not my desire for holiness, my ingenuity, or my desire to be cutting edge but my own fear of falling short that dictated this unmeasurable goal. After all, if the goal is unmeasurable, there is no missing it, and there would be no hot twinge of shame from the failure of missed goals. That self-awareness was lurking in the shadow recesses of my psyche but would take years to fully emerge and be named for what it was.

Be that as it may, now strangely liberated from the option of failure, we pledged ourselves to the new goal of being converted into the image of Christ. To be converted into his image would mean that we would experience what he had experienced and live what he had lived. He would be the way. We would know Christ in the biblical sense of the word and it was going to be great, holy, and cutting edge. It was a great plan, until we started to fail and suffer, until nobody came to worship with us, and we realized how much we really irritated each other. Until we began to experience at least part of what he had experienced and found out it was nothing at all what we wanted.

We fought with our desire for numeric success. For the first 4 years, the only words that seemed to come out of my mouth were, "That's not the goal." It wasn't the goal to advertise to draw people to worship with us. It wasn't our goal to get along with everyone. It wasn't our goal to be a big church. It wasn't our goal to have enough money to support a pastor. Only I wasn't sure if I was trying to convince them or myself as the loneliness of ministry and constant anxiety over the absence of numeric growth began to seep through the cracks.

Surely, we had missed expectations. We secretly couldn't wait to be big and to watch the masses profess our praise. We couldn't wait to succeed and show our parent congregations and the denomination we could make it on our own. We would have then surpassed not only their limited expectations of us, but potentially may have exceeded them as well (even though this was never our goal!). If only we could have named these demons in the beginning—demons that frankly haunt many new church starts. I've increasingly come to believe here that there wasn't much new or unique about our experience. It haunts the fringes of the new church start movement in North America.

I held on to "the goal" like a pit bull on a bone; the problem is you can't just decide one day to live into an entirely different world-view. We still wanted to be loved and acknowledged more than we wanted to know Christ. We wanted to win more than we wanted to fail. We wanted to experience the accolades of humans more than to experience Him and His loneliness, vulnerability, and smallness. All of which was the great irony . . . none of what we wanted was even closely associated to what Christ had experienced . . . none of what we wanted really had anything to do with our goal.

This, it turns out, would be our greatest challenge. We were a highly entrepreneurial group, as most people involved in such an endeavor are. We wanted to know we were succeeding. We *needed* to know we were doing something great for God. I was their leader, and I was just stepping out of corporate America and the traditional church—two organizations that measure success numerically. Would my ego be able to take it if no one found what we were doing attractive?

Four years into the project I was sent a warning, this quote from Thomas Merton:

> *Do not depend on the hope of results. When you are doing the sort of work you have taken on, essentially an apostolic work, you may have to face the fact that your work will be apparently worthless and achieve no result at all, if not results opposite to what you expect. As you get used to this idea, you start more and more to concentrate not on the results but on the value, the rightness, the truth of the work itself. And there too a great deal has to be gone through, as gradually you struggle less and less for an idea and more and more for specific people . . . In the end, it is the reality of personal relationships that saves everything* (Shannon 1993).

Ironically, I was sent this quote by someone who had joined our mission several years after its inception. She was a chronic overachiever, and this had been sitting on her desk the entire time she was attempting to prove her value to the world through what she could accomplish. She would be reflective of our first 4 years together as we said one thing, all the while our egos (at least my ego*) were screaming for something else.

> *This is why so many of these narcissists rise to positions of leadership. They get a lot of adulation, and as long as they get uncritical adulation, they can look very calm and self-assured. They are calm because they are getting adored, but when criticism comes, their world begins to disintegrate. When the truth comes out, then everything begins to fragment* (Moore 2003, 112).

A MONUMENT TO ME, PLEASE . . .

After a colossal failure in your field or in life, shame can encourage any number of reactions. I'm sure shame has encouraged many pastors of failed churches to never return—forever burnt on people, the church, God, or all of the above and the pain associated with those things. In other people, shame can insist we get back on the horse we fell off of to re-prove ourselves to the world. Those like me need to find some way of avoiding reality of failure by re-investing yourself someplace that will somehow reinforce the idea that you are enough, that you are more than enough. Perhaps it's not at all unlike the rebound boyfriend or girlfriend we feel obligated to find to prove to ourselves and our previous companion that we have value.

Fortunately for me, no one wanted me in ministry, so I was left to wander in the darkness in order to find my way out. This was

---

* As I re-read this. I see that I am collectively throwing the entire launch team in with my items of "our" hopes and dreams and "our" sense of failure. Looking back with more self-awareness, I still believe that's how it was, but I am prepared also to believe it was, at least in part, my own narcissistic projection—not wanting to be alone in my shame.

fortunate because what I didn't realize at the time was that the answers I needed were actually in the darkness in which I resided.

John Bradshaw—the author of that best-selling book on shame I mentioned earlier—retells the story of the prisoner in the dark cave (2005, 150):

> There once was a man who was sentenced to die. He was blind-folded and put in a pitch dark cave. The cave was 100 yards by 100 yards. He was told that there was a way out of the cave, and if he could find it, he was a free man.
>
> After a rock was secured at the entrance of the cave, the prisoner was allowed to take his blindfold off and roam freely in the darkness. He was to be fed only bread and water for the first 30 days and nothing thereafter. The bread and water were lowered from a small hole in the roof at the south end of the cave. The ceiling was about 18 feet high. The opening was about one foot in diameter. The prisoner could see a faint light up above, but no light came into the cave.
>
> As the prisoner roamed and crawled around the cave, he bumped into rocks. Some were rather large. He thought that if he could build a mound of rocks and dirt that was high enough, he could reach the opening and enlarge it enough to crawl through and escape. Since he was 5'9," and his reach was two feet, the mound had to be at least 10 feet high.
>
> So the prisoner spent his waking hours picking up rocks and digging up dirt. At the end of two weeks, he had built a mound of about six feet. He thought that if he could duplicate that in the next two weeks, he could make it before his food ran out. But as he had already used most of the rocks in the cave, he had to dig harder and harder. He had to do the digging with his bare hands. After a month had passed, the mound was nine and a half feet high, and he could almost reach the opening if he jumped. He was almost exhausted and extremely weak.

One day, just as he thought he could touch the opening, he fell. He was simply too weak to get up, and in two days, he died. His captors came to get his body. They rolled away the huge rock that covered the entrance. As the light flooded into the cave, it illuminated an opening in the wall of the cave about three feet in circumference.

The opening was the opening to a tunnel that led to the other side of the mountain. This was the passage to freedom the prisoner had been told about. It was in the south wall directly under the opening in the ceiling. All the prisoner would have had to do was crawl about 200 feet, and he would have found freedom. **He had so completely focused on the opening of light that it never occurred to him to look for freedom in the darkness. Liberation was there all the time right next to the mound he was building, but it was in the darkness.**

Three years after entering that darkness, I was given a straw of hope. I was asked by a friend to apply for a position as the lead pastor starting another church in our area. I applied for the position but voiced a particular concern:

A concern [I have] is that I may confuse a calling with an opportunity for redemption. While I don't doubt the Kingdom value of what is being attempted here, I only want to be a part if it truly is a calling and not part of my own desire for redemption within the denomination I love—a false attempt to redeem myself and save face. I realize redemption is an act of God alone, and I must guard against hope of retrieving that from human institutions.

I didn't want to keep digging my shame hole. I never got an interview. The person in charge of the team told me I was too old. That'll make the shame kick up, too!

They launched with a younger guy with a couple young kids.

Within in a year the church was dead, and I was again in the battle of the soul. While my heart broke for the guy because I know the loneliness of that failure, I was, at the same time, relieved. Why is it that we are pleased at the failure of others? Shame. There it was. Part of me needed him to fail to make me feel good about myself.

It's here that the other voice of shame enters the picture: self-contempt. I consider what a horrible person I am for being grateful for ill befalling a fellow human being so that I could find some redemption. What kind of person does that? Soon, I have castigated myself to the point of being "sub"-human, even though it really is just another expression of my actual humanness that I've been trying so hard to avoid.

Two years later, I was sitting with a group of denominational leadership. They too were attempting to discern if it were time for me to rejoin ministry. I told them I was instructed 2 years ago that I was too old for such an endeavor and that in the last 2 years I hadn't gotten any younger.

They asked me about the ministry I had previously launched. They asked what it did well. I heard a voice inside me telling me to lie, to tell a better tale than what actually happened. I didn't need to lie, directly.

Some in the group who knew me began to tell tales of my greatness that were clearly exaggerated. I'm not sure why they needed to exaggerate their tales for the denominational head who was there, but they did. And, while they did, I sat silent and not objecting to any of it.

When it was my turn, I too entered in with embellishments with regard to our success in attracting unchurched people and how effective we were at getting them to join the church. But I also withheld information that might reveal my weaknesses, such as the story about F bombing members of my congregation at a small group meeting. It seems like that would be something the denominational folks would want to know about.

I failed to enter the battle, shame won, and the hole got deeper. I knew it was going on as it was happening. In that moment, I had an opportunity to take a hit from the bottle of shame and my defense mechanisms came to my rescue so I made ready use of them. I was nowhere near as productive as I led him to believe.

Based on those lies, the denominational leadership said they *needed me.* They needed someone who had the ability to speak to people living outside the church the way I could. He started talking about how vital my skill set was to the success of the organization and that it was time they began to recognize the value of people like me. He said how important it was going to be to find a place for me and that maybe the denominational leaders who had described me as "too old" needed to be held accountable.

My soul was awash with relief. They loved me. They wanted me. Not only that, there was someone to blame for not choosing me for the other job! As they were speaking, I was flooded with endorphins of happiness. But, it wasn't *me* they wanted, it was who I was pretending to be—it was the false self we collectively generated in that short time over lunch. It was the self that was beyond limits, who was "more than enough" in every possible regard. After 5 years of floundering in the darkness and becoming so self-aware, it took just a few strokes from the right folks for the false self to return in a rush.

Then the main denominational guy (who was still singing my praises as all this was going through my head) ended on the following quote, "We should be building monuments to guys like you." I kid you not, those were his exact words.

This is where the spell broke for me. I looked him in the eye, and I described how good that felt to my shame-based false self. I described how I wanted nothing more in this world than that someone would build a monument in my honor. However, I said, I have learned the destructive power of those manipulative forces in my life and that I wasn't going to be seduced by them *in this particular moment.*

I got in my truck and drove home to feed the cattle who seemed oblivious to my greatness.

Perhaps tomorrow I would be weaker but, for today, I was strong. And today is all I have. This moment.

They determined that they were going to find a place for me anyway. I determined that I needed to keep walking past the bar, lest I be called in to drink deeply from that which I'm addicted. The lunch was over. I got in my truck and drove home to feed the cattle who seemed oblivious to my greatness. Farming always has a way of reminding me I'm not God.

> So whenever that brittle voice of dissatisfaction emerges within me, I can say "Ah, my ego! There you are, old friend!" It's the same thing when I'm being criticized and I notice myself reaching with outrage, heartache, or defensiveness. It's just my ego, flaring up and testing its power. In such circumstances, I have learned to watch my heated emotions carefully, but I try not to take them too seriously, because I know that it's merely my ego that has been wounded—never my soul It is merely my ego that wants revenge, or to win the biggest prize. It is merely my ego that wants to start a Twitter war against a hater, or to sulk at an insult or to quit in righteous indignation because I didn't get the outcome I wanted (Gilbert 2016, 244).

THE HIDDEN DAMAGE OF FEAR

I was not afraid of adopting our four kids. The bottom line with them is I realized they were pretty damaged when we got them. I knew I really couldn't do much worse than what they had experienced before they got to me. In the adoption of our kids, there was no real fear of exposure. There was no real opportunity at being exposed as a failure since the kids were all broken before I got them.

Starting the church was a different matter than choosing to raise the kids. I was afraid of failure there. Writing this book is a different matter as well—I could fail there on my own, too. Failure in endeavors that you bring into existence yourself offers the opportunity to say something about *you* personally. This is the failure we fear— because it says something about us personally.

The sensation of fear has one felt goal: to protect you. Its goal is to protect you from any number of things that you will experience as pain. However, the *way* fear protects you from pain is the sad scenario that becomes self-destructive; in this regard, shame is indeed a "wolf in sheep's clothing" (Thompson 93). This kind of fear could prevent people from getting married, having kids, writing books, public speaking, or speaking at all for that matter. This kind of fear will prevent us from experiencing the possibility of failure and the freedom that will, ultimately, come from that. Fear, in short, will simply prevent us from the living the life we want to live and that will ultimately be good for us and the rest of society.

> *Failure in endeavors that you bring into existence yourself offers the opportunity to say something about you personally.*

It's commonly understood by most leaders in the field of shame that the primary antidote for shame is vulnerability—to recapture what shame originally took from us (if you follow the ideas from Garden of Eden story). The intent of fear is to prevent you from being vulnerable and thus experiencing the potential pain of that vulnerability. Sadly, as mentioned, if "being vulnerable" is the only path toward healing, then fear is actually the primary defense mechanism shame wields from being expelled from your body.

Also, to protect itself from being discovered, it may actually generate more "symptoms" to lead you off track from finding and disarming this ingenious virus. It has become such a part of our lives we are no longer aware it even exits. It's not until we attempt to deal with the little rascal that we begin to see how deeply it is really dug into us.

As I mentioned earlier, my son and another friend of mine describe its work as an animate beast with tentacles into our soul. These two men understand how "dug in" the shame virus can be while remaining elusive. They also describe how it will actually go into hiding to an extent, only to resurface all the stronger later in life. While it is dug in deep, it prefers you not to be aware of its presence.

My Old Testament professor in seminary would tell the story of being out for a bike ride with his young son on a beautiful sunny fall afternoon. He lives in Holland, Michigan, where you can't swing a dead cat without hitting a church, the roads are all 25 mph, and air stinks of safety.

He and his small boy headed out, and my professor was struck by the stillness of the ride, the peacefulness, such that peddling was effortless. As such, they rode farther and farther than they had gone in the past, lost in the gentleness of the afternoon.

When my professor finally decided it was time to head home, he and his boy turned around to discover why things had been so peaceful and still: there was the slightest breeze pushing them along, which was about to become their worst nightmare. He knew it would be a challenge for his boy to get back home at this point and that they would have to battle this previously invisible force their entire way back to where they had begun.

This is where we find ourselves in this story as well. It's time we turn up wind and it will likely be a struggle against things that we may not even have been aware were having such an impact on our trajectory before now. As we turn our attention to the magnitude of the task that lay before us, I remind you in advance that both Jesus and M. Scott Peck called it "the road less traveled" for a reason.

If you are not willing to struggle, it is best that you just .... take your medication and forget about it, because struggle is reality.
—Robert Moore (2003, 18)

THE ROAD LESS TRAVELED

Life is difficult . . . —M. Scott Peck (1978, 15)

These are the first words of my favorite book and the first words I think of when I consider my eldest daughter, Tilonda, and the battle she knows she's in. I think of Tilonda because of the lunch we just had together when she wondered how long this struggle would last, but then I just as easily see myself in her question.

When I first read these words, I was struck by the simplicity of such a global reality, which I think was Dr. Peck's goal: to clobber us awake with a simple, global reality. Regardless of your religion, gender, age, or race, this is *the* all-encompassing truth of existence. In fact, it even felt odd to have to quote M. Scott Peck with words we all know to be true.

There's a good reason that book was a resounding best seller: it taps into this global reality. However, I wonder if it would sell today like it did when it was introduced because it is clearly *not* a how-to book. There are no easy steps to the sort of transformation offered in his seminal book on living a truly healthy life.

Even accepting the opening phrase, "Life is difficult," itself is a struggle for me. It's taken me some time and effort in life to embrace this little confession that life is difficult. I still have a tendency, as Dr. Peck suggests, to "moan more or less incessantly, noisily or subtly, about the enormity of (my) problems, (my) burdens, and (my) difficulties as if life were generally easy, as if life *should* be easy" (p. 15).

Right from the beginning, the challenge Dr. Peck offers us in his book is the opportunity to embrace reality—to live by the truth to the fullest extent that it can possibly be done without causing irreparable harm to others. While Dr. Peck's book is not expressly about dealing with shame, his challenge to "live by truth" will lead us full force into being vulnerable because "truth telling" is what shame is attempting to protect you from doing. Telling the truth, living by the truth, is the principal avenue leading to vulnerability—the place scholars on shame insist we must arrive for any hope of healing.

LESSONS FROM THE ITALIAN STALLION

Like many kids growing up in the '70s, I spent a good deal of life living vicariously through Rocky Balboa. I guess I probably still do. He had an ability to get every person in a room on their feet at the end of his fights believing they could take on the world and win. Rocky had a way of suspending reality—the idea that we were just watching a movie—to give us an opportunity to enter into a possibility.

If you grew up in my generation watching this movie, we know that we all wanted to jump to our feet as Rocky, in snowy Philadelphia, ascended the steps of the Philadelphia Museum of Art, believing we too could conquer the obstacles that lay before us. However, we could not nor did we want to spend the individual moments of battle that got him there. That is our challenge. There is no glory there. No one will probably know other than you. But transformation of a soul, the rewriting of a life script, happens one line at a time, and we have to be prepared for the long, slow process of doing the writing.

So, this is what I promised to offer at the beginning of this book: an invitation to the fight to take back control of your script.

The small pieces of this fight are a fight for awareness. An awareness of the battle with the person inside you who is insisting that you take one action based on the old scripts and negotiating with that person which decision you would make with a new script—the story you would write for yourself if you had the opportunity.

If we listen closely enough to ourselves, we can see those opportunities arising with almost every interaction we have with another person. McNish warns pastors of this reality in this way:

"If we are attentive we hear shame in our parishioners' anguish over loss of jobs, loss of relationships, failures in child rearing, addictions of all kinds, the aging process, even illness . . . can we provide the sense of 'deep calling to deep' that people need in times when they want their shame to be heard even as they couch it in expressions of rage, contempt, depression, or righteousness? This depends in no small part on the honesty with which we ourselves confront our own demons, our own shame issues" (McNish 2004, 83)

My own demons were evident throughout my ministry, preventing me from hearing the trauma involved in the lives of my own congregants. Since that failure, however, I have been able to see my own demons and my own shame issues. This has allowed me to engage more deeply with how this force is affecting those around me in life—most notably my children.

I have a goal for my kids: that they have the ability and will to enter this fight to take back their lives from the shame that has controlled their lives, as it has my own. I want nothing more than for my kids to bravely be themselves in this world but can offer them no easy path to that point.

To be nobody-but-yourself in a world which is doing its best, night and day, to make you everybody but yourself- means to fight the hardest battle which any human being can fight – and never stop fighting. —e. e. cummings (1955)

ENTERING REALITY

The truth shall set you free, but first it will make you miserable.
— Unknown

I was recently leading a Skype meeting for the management of our organization to review the condition of one of the businesses I'm managing for my employer. It's quite apparent that the business is struggling, as is much of the industry we serve. It's part of my responsibility to help resolve this and bring the business back to strength.

The first step is acknowledging the condition we're in, consuming about half of my PowerPoint slide deck. It's not an easy task to acknowledge things are not going well, and, at first, we tend to hope the declines are something of an illusion. Initially, we may want to sugarcoat the situation a bit, with ourselves and our coworkers. But eventually, you have to face reality that things are not well if you want to get beyond the present state. So, as I said, the first half of my deck was to welcome people into "reality"—perhaps a reality they too were avoiding.

> *The idea here is that we all hope that there's an easy way out, that we won't actually have to work and sacrifice to become what we want.*

The challenge? The second half of the deck of slides involved deciding what we're going to do about it. It's at this time that the oft-quoted phrase, "Hope is not a strategy," arrives. The idea here is that we all hope that there's an easy way out, that we won't actually have to work and sacrifice to become what we want.

This is as much true with our human condition as it is with any other sphere of our lives. The idea of not being motivated and manipulated any longer by this hidden driver called *shame* may be a very attractive idea. Being the kind of person who can live their own life and not the life being dictated to them by their baggage and fears may seem like an off-the-charts outstanding idea. But that does very little to get us there. To get there will take hard work.

So, now it's time to face the dragon.

CHAPTER 7

Facing the Dragon

Here's the [short] version of Jung's model. In youth, we assemble a persona, a public face that helps us get along, cope with junior high, trick women into bed, and the boss into giving raises. Behind this mask, we suppress all our neuroses, dreads, and the stuff that's too dark, artistic, or just plain odd for polite company.

As long as things go well, this works. But once the persona starts screwing up (e.g., lets us get fired or divorced), all those stifled secrets, once willing to shut up, start shouting up from the basement. The only answer, wrote Jung, is to turn directly toward the approaching darkness and "find out what it wants from you" (O'Neill 2003).

SEAT 11A

It was the spring of 2016 and I was looking out over the green pastures of my farm, the envy of many who would come here to buy a bull from me and many others. Visitors, friends, even contractors working on my house—who had a romantic inner desire to get out of the office and routine of life to work with their hands in the fields—would often recount for me how lucky I am.

I agreed, philosophically and cognitively, which left all the more mystery around the misery and depression in my own soul, my failure to find any joy or happiness in my life. After years of medication and counseling, I had made little long-term progress at finding joy (and not much short-term progress as far as that goes). In fact, I became more prone to lashing out in anger and rage against myself and anything that exposed my inner turmoil.

On this particular day, overlooking my fields, I came (again) to the realization that I could not live this way. I was not suicidal, although what I am describing may seem to suggest it. I was acknowledging that living my life in this darkness was unsustainable, that it was not living at all.

A couple of weeks later I was on a plane to central Wisconsin— American Airlines flight 3493, seat 11A—that I realized God wasn't going to help remove my plight from me. I was on my own to sort this out. Ironically, it was an exit row seat.

I was on my way to yet another district sales meeting. Steeped again in my own despair, doubt, and self-pity, I realized that God wasn't coming to change my circumstances or heal my broken psyche. God wasn't coming to offer me a way out of the restlessness and turmoil to take me to some place that didn't exist. I had studied the likes of the apostle Paul, Mother Teresa, and Henri Nouwen enough to realize that if He didn't do it for those great contributors to His Kingdom, He wasn't about to do it for this chemical engineer turned failed church planter returned chemical engineer.

Restlessness is part of our lot. Futility is part of our lot. Darkness is our companion. So, there I was in seat 11A. Exit row. About to land at Central Wisconsin Airport with a renewed understanding that I was alone, just like everyone else.

Ironically, God leaves us alone at some point. C.S. Lewis portrayed this idea that God would step back out of our conscious view, and he compared God to parents who remove their hands from their toddler and applaud with glee at his or her feeble attempts to walk. All of that going through the mind of the guy in 11A.

Like most of my religious colleagues, I had come under the mistaken impression that God existed to make my life better. How and when we get that impression, I'm not sure, but it's an impression without any substantial validation throughout the Bible and throughout the history of the church.

> *I had come under the mistaken impression that God existed to make my life better.*

If there's anything the modern church has intended to teach it's that Jesus is the way. What this has come to mean is that he must be accepted into our hearts (whatever that means), and we must believe he has forgiven our sins. "The way," then, has become the path to heaven—the ticket to the really, really good life following a time on earth when we get most of our requests granted from His highness anyway.

Instead, I wonder what Jesus *meant* when he said that anyone not willing to pick up his or her own cross and follow him—to follow HIS way—would not be worthy of him. In his teaching, Jesus says again and again that he is the way. Henri Nouwen was one who understood this clearly. There is no way to the Father other than the way of Jesus, the way of suffering, sacrifice, and struggle. All of which somehow became synonymous with "the way of love."

Still, sitting in seat 11A, I was overcome with a desire that God do *something* to make my life "better." This sort of whining is likely what drove M. Scott Peck to open his epic book *A Road Less Traveled* with these words: "Life is hard—quit complaining and solve it" (a gratuitous summation on my behalf).

I had hoped seat 11A would go down in history as a pivot point for me—for better or worse. It has not. Six months later, in seat 6A on the way to Little Rock, the darkness and uncertainty persisted. The only certainty I have is that God is unlikely to come to my aid, because in the midst of this darkness I am apparently "on the way."

When my own personal suffering from depression could no longer be set aside, I returned to counseling and the search for medication. While the medication route did not appear to offer any salvation once again, a book my therapist gave me did help and moved me toward an understanding that would shift how I functioned in the world. That book was by Chicago Theological Seminary professor Robert L. Moore and was titled, appropriately, *Facing the Dragon: Confronting Personal and Spiritual Grandiosity*.

This is what needed to happen in my life. I needed to "turn to the darkness and find out what it wanted from me." I needed to face the dragon and confront my personal and spiritual grandiosity—my shame-based need for being great.

Moore's book helped me understand something in my life that was buried deep in my psyche, "grandiosity." Grandiosity is a narcissistic defense mechanism I frequently experienced that was somehow suggesting in me that I "deserved" better treatment—that I deserved more recognition, that I deserved to be happy. Because I was not getting what I "deserved," the anger and depression grew.

Moore's book also helped me understand the power of shame in my life as it was expressing itself through grandiosity. He personifies it and calls it the dragon, the demonic, or Lucifer. In his book, Moore says that "the demonic is closer than you think" (Moore 2003, 1). These words hit me hard and challenged me to look at my own life in a new way. I began to wonder how close this demonic force of shame really was in my life and how much control did it really have over me.

The Lucifer complex, as Moore describes it, exists beyond cultures, religions, and races.

"In some cultures, this toxic alien presence is conceptualized as demons, in others as idolatry, in others as the power of temptations of illusion and desire. This presence usually promises both significance of desire, the eclipse of limitations, and the ability to become the center of the world" (Moore 2003, 9).

People struggling with shame are very susceptible to promises of significance, power, and the ability to overcome any limitation. In fact, the ability to overcome limitations is what was suggested to Eve in the garden by the snake. Who would not want to be the center of the world (even though we know we could never get there without the help of our false self)?

Moore emphasized a pressing and urgent need to *understand* "the great solar fires that operate unconsciously within us to drive the increasing epidemics of personal and social *evil*" (2003, 1).

I emphasized the word "understand" because acknowledging the present reality is the starting point to making progress in life—disarming this enemy within cannot happen until we acknowledge its existence and it will never happen if we just wallow in our grief in whatever seat we happen to be in at the moment.

> *... disarming this enemy within cannot happen until we acknowledge its existence.*

I emphasized the word "evil" because it's the word that most closely aligns with what we are doing to ourselves personally and corporately.

People who cannot admit they have a permanent problem with their tendencies toward pathological grandiosity are simply deluding themselves, and they become part of the larger human problem. We all need to take part in the human recovery project (Moore 2003, 189).

I can tell you from my experience that grandiosity—this reaction to internal shame—leads to personal and social destruction.

I remember vividly the chants of the Episcopalian worship service I attended weekly as a child where we asked for forgiveness for "things done" as well as "things left undone," and we were well aware that both things could be forms of "evil." What I am proposing here is that they are both sourced in shame. As Curt Thompson noted, "It starts and (surprisingly) ends wars, only to start them again. It fuels injustice and creates our excuses for doing little if anything about it" (2015, 9).

As you've already probably picked up from me after reading this far, I believe *the first step in entering into this battle is to realize we are in one.* That there is *something* lurking causing us to be and do what we do not want.

> *For indeed, [shame] is everywhere, and there is virtually nothing left untainted by it. From our family at home to the one at church. From the bedroom to the boardroom. From school to work to play. From the art studio to the science and technology lab* (Thompson 2015, 9).

I've already mentioned the Deming principle made famous by Peter Drucker: *"You can't change what you don't measure."*

The principle is largely a challenge to understand your present situation as a basic background for moving beyond where you are to where you want to be, especially if you don't like where you presently reside. For example, you can't find a way to increase sales if you don't understand what's inhibiting your ability to grow sales. You can't find a way to cut costs until you actually know what your costs are.

The same is frequently understood for managing your own personal financial situation or weight loss or overcoming an addiction. Much can be accomplished to improve your financial situation by creating a budget and watching that budget, or tracking your calories to understand what you're eating. Most people have no idea how much they spend in certain areas (or eat) until they actually start recording it.

The insidious thing about shame is that it's hidden within and was once necessary for our survival. *The "enemy within" was once our protector and survival mechanism and has become literally the water in which we are swimming.* The problem? We are drowning and don't know why. Moore said it this way:

> *If you don't have some sense of the warfare going on inside you at the psychological level, then you will be less able to do what you need to do to free yourself from the things try-ing to drag you down and imprison you and stifle your life* (Moore 2003, 16).

ACKNOWLEDGE THE FIRES WITHIN

Naming something inherently removes its power. It's why the first statement at an Alcoholics Anonymous meeting involves naming the truth: I am an alcoholic. Calling something out of the shadows and looking at it is the only way out of this.

When my son, Troy, came asking for help to deal with "the fires within," I told him that the battle, although seemingly insurmount-able at the moment, was already half won by simply being able to acknowledge the situation. I also applauded the fact that at 29 years of age, he was already 100% more self-aware than I was at his age, which, I can only imagine, is a good thing.

My son was also able to show me how linked the psychological idea of "grandiosity" and shame are—that shame is the source of what Robert Moore was getting at. Finally, my son reminded me of the most important thing: I am not alone.

Naming something inherently removes its power.

If you've read this far in this book, you've probably come to realize, like my son, that something in your life isn't working. This doesn't make you a freak, it makes you actually rather normal and consistent with the great majority of humanity. If anything about this revelation you're having makes you unique it's that you have the courage to admit it. That, in itself, is a substantial achievement and puts you in rather good company.

John Bradshaw is a hugely successful author and therapist with a number of best sellers, television appearances, programs, awards, and a distinguished teaching career all on his resume. Yet, even here, shame lurks. In his seminal book—his 1.3 million-copy-selling *Healing the Shame that Binds You*—he opens with this confession:

> *Ten years ago . . . I named the core demon in my life. I named 'shame.' This means that I became aware of the massive destructive power shame had exerted in my life. I discovered that I had been bound by shame all my life. It ruled me like an addiction. I acted it out; I covered it up on subtle and not-so-subtle ways; I transferred it to my family, my clients and the people I taught.*

> *Shame was the unconscious demon I had never acknowledged. In becoming aware of the dynamics of shame, I came to see that shame is one of the major destructive forces in all human life. In naming shame I began to have power over it* (Bradshaw 1988, xvii).

It should not surprise us that these forces lurk in any of us, regardless of how well it appears we have things together or how educated we are in understanding them. For example, it is well known that M. Scott Peck was himself challenged to walk the road he prescribed for us, and I was devastated by the news of Dr. Moore's demise—particularly the nature of it—as were many whose lives were so positively impacted by his work. I added him to my list of authors whose work was so inspirational to me—Alice Miller, as well—who were able to communicate the inner truths of how we end up where we end up but were also constantly running from their own demons at the same time.

BATTLING SHAME REQUIRES UNDERSTANDING THE ENEMY

"If you know the enemy and know yourself, you need not fear the result of a hundred battles. If you know yourself but not the enemy, for every victory gained you will also suffer a defeat. If you know neither the enemy nor yourself, you will succumb in every battle." —Sun Tzu, *The Art of War*

When you're looking at an approach to becoming resilient to shame, it's been helpful for me to see shame in an animated way, not like an emotion or something I feel. Shame is not guilt and shame is not embarrassment. I tend to speak of shame in terms of a virus with a mind and will of its own. You've probably sensed me doing that throughout this book, and I hear it in the words from other authors such as Curt Thompson (2015):

It likes to do its work and, when exposed, retreat into the shadows, only then to remerge no less potently than before (p. 11).

It's also important to remember that you are likely *working together with* the virus because it has you convinced you need it for your protection against some perceived pain. Therefore, we, ourselves, have mixed motives when it actually comes to getting beyond the situation. In fact, it will be quick to remind you of your need for its protection. It's therefore frequently hard to discern if this thing called shame is actually friend or foe.

If we are to take our struggle seriously in this way, we must understand what we are dealing with—its method of operation and its chief objectives.

The first time I did a national radio interview, it was on the subject of narcissism—particularly as it pertained to how the term was in constant use relative to Donald Trump and his run for the presidency.

It was my goal in that interview to shed some light on the fact that shame is the underbelly of narcissism and that, although people were seeing Donald Trump as arrogant and egotistical and dangerous in his arrogance, I wanted to suggest that "arrogance" was not the issue. I was suggesting he was actually steeped in self-hatred causing him to generate this front as the greatest human being ever—that it was his low sense of self that required him to present himself to us as our savior.

I wanted to argue that the real danger of such a person was their ability to be manipulated in exchange for adoration, and I believed we were already seeing the beginnings of that in his relationship with Russian President Vladimir Putin.

The problem: I found out just prior to going on the show that the host was a *huge* Trump fan. Ugh! I also found that he was a very challenging and very thorough host—being largely fair but not letting his guests off the hook very easily. Again, Ugh! I made it to his first question before I felt the red-hot surge of shame:

"Are you a psychologist?" he asked.

What he was really asking was, "*What qualifies you to speak on this matter??*" It's a very reasonable question, but that's not how it felt when it hit me.

To me, it was a body blow. It was my worst fear when wading into this endeavor: that it would be discovered that I was a fraud, and he wanted *that* question answered out of the chute! Am I a fraud? Again, it's a reasonable question.

Looking back, I needed to take the host at face value with his question. It's a valid question. Even though he was asking a fair and legitimate question, what I heard was, "What the hell do you know anyway?" and shame demanded I defend myself. That's what shame does—it pretends to come to your aid against your potential exposure.

It's in moments like this, as you are experiencing the pain of exposure and vulnerability after having let down your defenses, that your inner critic is quick to speak up. When feeling exposed, as I was, your inner critic will remind you that you are experiencing this pain because you attempted to set him (your inner critic) aside. Shame (via your inner critic) will then say things like, "I told you this was stupid!! How could you be so stupid? Goddamn, man, you just took a direct hit and you're going down! Abandon ship!!" The whole time reminding you that you are too stupid to go through life without its protection.

My inner critic is also then very good at conjuring up some defense strategies. Like "run," for example, or "fight." I typically choose fight (big surprise for people who have read this far!!), but in the example I gave about my radio interview, "run" seemed a more logical defense but pretending to lose phone connectivity and hanging up seemed like a third grade thing to do. I felt a need to defend myself even though my "attacker" had a legitimate right to know the basis on which I was claiming expertise in this matter.

Right here and right now, it's important to know the enemy and know what it is trying to do. It is attempting to derail your opportunity at vulnerability. It is attempting to prevent and diminish your opportunity for failure. It is attempting to shout you down and shut you up before you have a real opportunity to simply be yourself and be honest, win, lose, or draw.

With the red hot venom of shame coursing through my veins coming to "rescue me" from my humiliation, I chose to fight for my right to be vulnerable. I chose the opportunity for failure. I chose to be myself. I opted for the truth. I say "opted," which makes me sound brave. I don't think I had a choice. I had been discovered. It was time, as Carl Jung might say, for me to "face the darkness and find out what it wants from me."

"No," I said. "I'm not a psychologist. I have a Master's of Divinity and a Doctor of Ministry degree but no psychology degree. Most of my training in narcissism has been through these experiences combined with my day jobs in the pastorate and corporate America. Most importantly," I said, "I'm a recovering narcissist myself."

I had made that argument over and over in my doctoral dissertation—that the best person to speak on alcoholism is a recovering alcoholic, and the person who most understands that the underbelly of narcissism is shame, is a recovering narcissist. However valid *that* argument sounded before this moment, I felt like a big turd as the words came out of my mouth in *this* moment.

Well, I'm no psychologist. I'm a new business development manager for a chemical company. I'm an ordained minister who doesn't go to church. I'm a farmer trying to keep 50 head of cattle alive. I'm a father of four adopted African American kids. And, I'm a recovering narcissist. Primarily, I'm a human being. In all those experiences, I've paid particular attention to how we make our decisions and how we chose our courses. And, frankly, those realities make me an expert in how shame attempts to shape our lives.

> *Standing up for yourself without being defensive. Stepping into an opportunity to flounder. Preparing to tell the truth. Fighting the urge to run or embellish. Exposing yourself to potential failure. These are tools we use to combat the enemy within.*

Standing up for yourself without being defensive. Stepping into an opportunity to flounder. Preparing to tell the truth. Fighting the urge to run or embellish. Exposing yourself to potential failure. These are tools we use to combat the enemy within.

Most all experts agree that the goal in our battle with shame (once you acknowledge you're in a battle) boils down to this willingness to become vulnerable. We need to go where the enemy does not want us to go, which will make shame come out of hiding and present itself.

A better way to say it is to acknowledge that we, as human organisms, are foundationally vulnerable creatures. And key to becoming resilient to shame is to walk headlong into that reality. Open yourself to the possibility of being hurt so you can discover that you are no longer a child in need of protection from pain, that you can withstand it on your own, get through it, learn from it, and grow.

What you'll find is it's challenging to do that apart from other people (especially sharp radio hosts!!); it's when we are around other people that shame really has a strong opportunity to raise its voice to defend us from humiliation. Although we can feel self-humiliation, as I did when I tripped over my shoes in the field, we are most apt to feel "humiliated" when exposed to and looking bad in front of others. Being around people is the easiest way to generate shame-inducing situations. This is why shame wants us isolated. This is why shame wants us alone. This is the battleground on which we fight.

If we are going to address this issue in our lives, we must have a plan. We should not attempt to avoid shame, as it can't seemingly be done, and, by avoiding it, we allow it to leverage us from the shadows. Instead, as Kaufman says, we need to understand it and how best to cope with it while paying respect to its "dynamic role in human development, and how profound can be its aftermath" (Kaufman 1992, 77).

CHAPTER 8

Join the Club

Shame confronts us with a profound sense of isolation from others, with our aloneness in the world (Capps 1993, 81).

*The by-products of shame—fear, blame, and **disconnection*** (Brown 2008, xiv).

P art of knowing the enemy is to understand its chief goal is to isolate. You cannot fight this battle in isolation because, while you are there, shame has already won.

WE ALL NEED A POKE

It was that time again. It was time to get that old, sick cow, #8279, up and walk her to the back of the pasture. She didn't want to move. She was battling a double-duty body blow—she had a

106.5-degree fever from toxic mastitis and had acidified her belly by eating too many oats. Truth be told, those were oats I fed her, so at least half of her problem I had induced myself.

It was unlikely she'd survive, but she had a month-old calf she still seemed to care about. Sadly, the two remaining good parts of her udder were now dry because she wasn't eating or drinking, so her baby calf was needing to be bottle-fed because it was starving as well.

She didn't want to move. She looked like death. I took it upon myself twice a day to go get her up and walk her to the back of the pasture, to remind her she was a cow, to remind her what cows do. On the way out, she would nibble at some grass, maybe paw some dirt. More out of instinct maybe than will. She would have preferred to stay laying in the mud. But she had to move. Once I got her to the back of the pasture, she would have to walk the 1,300 feet back to her calf. Seems cruel, but I knew she had to keep moving, or she would simply give up.

On this particular trip out to the back of the pasture, I wondered who was saving who. I realized the poetic nature of our trips to the back of the pasture, as it too brought me up out of my depression and anger to simply do what needed to be done in that moment. As she and I walked to the back of the pasture together—her with her toxic mastitis–induced fever and empty, soured, belly and me with my depression-laden psychic fever and empty, soured, soul—I realized I had a partner in survival, me and old #8279.

As we walked out to the back pasture together, I carried a stick with which to give her a gentle poke when she started slowing down. I knew we couldn't stop moving because if we did, we'd be done altogether.

Poke, a few more steps. Poke, a few more steps. Little did she know that she was poking me as well, in my hope to keep her alive.

This is probably step number one in walking this road less traveled: finding someone to walk with. Shame insists we walk alone, in silence. Shame flourishes in silence. Shame is the *hidden* killer.

Together, with your partner, you can walk and poke, walk and poke, reminding yourselves that it is a difficult path to recovery but it requires movement; it requires slow deliberate actions that empower us to do what cows (humans) do—eat some grass, kick some dirt, and keep moving toward recovery. Go to work, raise your kids, do what needs to be done, aware that you are in a battle for your life. As Robert Moore knows well, "Evil wants to get you alone and isolate you. It also wants to get you in the dark" (2003, 37).

There is something intensely vital about finding a community of travelers on this journey. I have two reasons for suggesting that to be the case:

1. **All the authors and experts on this subject unequivocally agree on this point. It's hard enough to get two people to agree on anything, but on this one thing, they agree.**
2. **I am walking this path—my own path—alone, and I realize it's not the way to do it. I realize this on a daily basis, so it is highest on my list to find a way to not only tell my own story but listen to others as well, to be in community on this issue.**

I found one thing clear without exception. When I am in conversation with people on these issues—particularly those who are fellow travelers—I am healed a little bit or at least sustained. I find conversation partners in the books I read as well as in the telling of this tale you now hold in your hand. I envision myself telling you of these struggles as if you are sitting here now and listening to me and, in doing so, you have brought me healing.

Shame insists you live alone. Becoming shame resilient alone is not possible. There is no other way to say it. You can look to all the modern researchers on

> *Becoming shame resilient alone is not possible. There is no other way to say it.*

shame or the account in Genesis itself to show you that shame is the fear of being exposed, and perhaps the summation of all shame defense mechanisms is to disconnect you from other people to whom you may be vulnerable.

Doing battle with shame requires you to *specifically and carefully* do the *opposite* of what shame is asking you to do. Doing battle with shame will require you to *specifically and carefully* become vulnerable to other human beings—perhaps, as a starter, by simply asking for help, as my son Troy did recently. Doing battle with shame requires that we attempt to take back what it has stolen from us—our opportunity to be in open and sincere relationships with other people and to be genuinely *ourselves* in those relationships. However, as #8279 and I can tell you, it's a long hard walk.

LET THE STARVATION BEGIN

"We do not execute shame quickly via some behavioral guillotine, but rather starve it out over time . . ." (Thompson 2015, 36).

It's not often you can get a group of scholars to agree on something. However, one thing I can attest to in my own work has already been discovered by the best in field: that this is a long process and there is no easy fix. *If we believe the lie that there's an easy way out of this mess, we misunderstand the virus we are battling* and how deeply the enemy is every part us as much as it is something else. In underestimating the enemy and our own role in aiding and abetting the enemy, we will never gain an upper hand. It's also important to note that the goal, as already mentioned, is not necessarily overcoming shame as much as it is coping with it. Brené Brown says it this way:

> *We can never become completely resistant to shame; however, we can develop the resilience we need to recognize shame, move through it constructively and grow from our experiences* (Brown 2008, xiv).

Unfortunately, we expect an easy life. We expect a fair life. We think we "deserve" such a thing. But this is our grandiosity talking. This thing we want or expect doesn't exist. It's an illusion, and living an aware life is a life constantly in battle over the illusions we generate for ourselves. Moreover, we've become accustomed to being offered and wanting quick fixes—which is another form of illusion. There's nothing more I would prefer to do here than to offer you, me, my kids a quick fix to this predicament. It simply does not exist. Even Jesus did not heal himself but walked the road less traveled to show us the way, the truth, and the life.

> *These scripts cannot easily be undone, nor can the venom be easily extracted. Perhaps they can never be undone. Our goal is to tame them. Our goal is to disarm them so they can't do us, or others, any further damage.*

Sadly, as I mentioned, these are the scripts that we have written for ourselves with the assistance of our collective but differentiated backgrounds and life experiences. This is the venom coursing through our veins. These scripts cannot easily be undone, nor can the venom be easily extracted. Perhaps they can never be undone. Our goal is to tame them. Our goal is to disarm them so they can't do us, or others, any further damage.

I have some strategies I've used to begin to own the process instead of it owning me. This list is not at all exhaustive. Now that you are becoming part of a community, that is most likely where you will find the strategies that best suit your situation. All of the strategies I suggest are aimed at bringing shame into the light because, once it's exposed, it cannot survive. It's important to start this process in Zorro circles.

ZORRO CIRCLES

I was speaking with a CEO recently who was attempting to change the culture of his organization—a task facing many CEOs new to their position.

His perception was that his organization had previously been run by fear—another situation common to many organizations. He was seeing the results of that; namely, people were unwilling to take risks or think or act for themselves. The culture of an organization is something built deep within itself, in its proverbial DNA, as much as our story is also written deep within ourselves. Change won't come quickly or easily.

The question, his question, is where to start and the answer is, someplace small.

In his book, *The Happiness Advantage*, Shawn Achor points us to the movie *The Mask of Zorro*. In that rendition, Zorro was not always the swashbuckler we've come to know. In fact, "by the time the aging sword master Don Diego meets him, [Zorro] is a broken man, a slave to drinking and despair. But Don Diego sees the young man's potential and takes him under his wing" (Achor 2011, 128).

The key to transformation that Don Diego brings to Alejandro (Zorro's actual name) is forcing him to master fighting first in a small circle—a circle that will be his whole world. Once that area is mastered, Don Diego draws ever-larger circles, building Alejandro's confidence until he has become who Don Diego always knew he was.

What I propose here is a series of Zorro circles: small steps that will empower a life of continued transformation and "success" as defined by becoming a person increasingly less manipulated by shame and fear.

All of the disciplines I've used have been intended to help me practice awareness of how shame is affecting my life. My belief and hope is that through practicing awareness, I will increase the likelihood of my transformation through this process.

What follows are some of my own Zorro circles.

STOP DIGGING

In 2013, the Pittsburgh Steelers started off in pretty rough shape having kicked off their season 0–4. Mike Tomlin, their coach, was asked how they intended to get out of the hole they were in. Mike's response to getting out of a hole was, "Well, first you have to stop digging."

As I mentioned at the beginning of this book, changing course on scripts that have been wired not only into us individually, but into humanity in general, is no easy task. However, the first thing we need to do once we are *aware* we are in a hole is to stop digging. Similar to being an alcoholic, the first task before you is the most monumental: stop drinking.

Sadly, this is not an easy path. You will find around nearly every interaction with another human the opportunity take a drink from the shame cup. With nearly every human interaction, you will be given an opportunity to raise your shame defenses to protect yourself from the pain of exposure and to keep digging that hole for yourself.

When we connect with individuals that engage our shame responses, we will want to take the shovel and begin digging again. It may even want to make us retreat to the greatest hole of them all: isolation. Instead, we need to find a way to engage those shame responses, refuse the shovel, and begin to build some steps *out* of the hole.

I commend Bradshaw's book for what appears to be a much more complete list of step-building tools and of the expanse of treatment and coping options before us—mechanisms I will likely be attempting to employ in my own life. For now, in my own life and in this book, I choose to stay focused on the line now made famous by the Bill Murray movie *What About Bob*: taking baby steps. One interaction at a time. One conversation at a time. One incident at a time. Looking for shame to raise its head so I can name it, shine light on it, and make my own decision. Anything bigger than that right now, and I'll likely stumble and fall.

USE OF EMPATHY AND DEVELOPMENT
OF COMPASSION

One of the hallmarks of building your way out of the shame condition is compassion. Brené Brown has made compassion and
empathy foundational building blocks for developing shame resilience (2008). For her, it seems, that compassion and empathy are
"the way, the truth, and the life." I name that "Jesus," but I think we
may actually be saying the same thing.

Compassion toward others for sure, but what may actually be
more difficult for people struggling with shame is to find compassion for yourself. If contempt or hatred for yourself and others is
the venom of shame, then empathy and compassion, the opposite of
contempt, must certainly be the anti-venom. Brené Brown has gone
so far as to declare empathy to be the ladder that brings us out of the
shame hole.

One of my invisible mentors in writing this book is the actress
Ariel Winter who plays Alex Dunphy on the sitcom *Modern Family*.
She seems to be repeatedly harassed by body shamers on social media
about what others perceive to be her physical imperfections. It's her
responses that I find fascinating. She repeatedly draws attention to
how her attackers must feel about themselves that make them have
to attack her in that way.

It makes me recall the guy who had verbally attacked my daughter in the gym that night and how, as I turned to beat him down, I
was held back by another man shouting, "He's not worth it" to me.
Certainly, he must have a shame-based condition to have to attack
a young African American teenager using her appearance as his
weapon of choice.

What if we existed in a world where we had the ability to pause
before we retaliated at people who hurt us and consider how they
too must be suffering to strike us that way? Would it prevent a
broken hand or a pastoral resignation when someone rolls their eyes

at us? Would it prevent scaring ourselves, the ones we love, or even innocent bystanders such that they will have new issues in their own lives to overcome? Is it possible that compassion and empathy could simply prevent all forms of retaliation and escalation?

It's hard to understand or appreciate your attacker in cases where *you* are the one being blamed or shamed in some way, as Ariel Winter seems to have mastered. But the source of the attack is without question the attacker's own shame they are attempting to hide by exposing yours. One of the great values that can come from a healthy understanding of how shame works is an appreciation for

> *What if we existed in a world where we had the ability to pause before we retaliated at people who hurt us and consider how they too must be suffering to strike us that way?*

what makes others do what they do. If this is done right, it can actually breed something called *empathy*—perhaps the greatest human achievement next to love.

Oddly, it may be compassion and empathy that the world needs more than any other social medication. I put this one first because it seems like it's the source of the others. The main question is, what is it about empathy and compassion that has such a powerful influence on positively engaging shame?

If you remember, the primary function of shame is to protect you from the perceived (and real) pain of the exposure of your imperfections and "not enoughness" to the world. The function of shame is 100% about *you*. Perhaps it's here you can also see the connection between shame and narcissism. Empathy is primarily about the other person or people. When you are being empathetic, there is a requirement that you engage the importance of another human being. This may cause shame to emerge for you to name and put back to bed but that is really the goal. Get it to raise its head so it can be acknowledged and informed that you are now in charge.

This, by the way, is also why empathy is such a powerful double-edged sword. Not only does it introduce you to the battle with your own shame, but it will also soothe the shame of the other person as they get a sense that maybe they matter in the world. If we can soothe the shame of another human being, perhaps they will have a diminished need to lash out the next time their own shame defenses are triggered. Perhaps, once soothed, they can offer their own empathy to another human being and change the trajectory for individual human lives.

Attempting to practice empathy, however, is not for the faint of heart. Some people I acknowledge are naturally brilliant at it. Others, like myself, not so much. It literally takes practice, especially when that empathy or compassion needs to be directed at your own self.

When I speak of having compassion on one's own self, I have to believe it's completely clear what I'm referring to. That said, it's an odd concept because it suggests there are at least three of you. The first of you is the small, weak, and insufficient you—the failure—and the one constantly risking getting the rest of you embarrassed or humiliated in their smallness and stupidity.

Another "you" is also there that presses their will on the smaller and weaker you to get that "you" to shut up, keep your head down, and keep walking. That stronger you—the "you police"—is also the first one at the scene when you've screwed up to remind you not only that you *have* screwed up but also that you *are* a screw-up. Now, if we keep in mind that this "you" is actually just trying to keep the whole you from feeling the pain of being exposed, you've really come to believe it's in your best interest to beat the weaker you into submission.

The growing dilemma is that, it seems to me, there must be another you—a third you—that shows up at the scene to make peace. Initially to protect the smaller you but then to help the stronger you stand down—to learn from failure and loss and mistakes so that, as a group, we all can become the best possible, most mature, well-adjusted, and societally contributive "you" possible. The goal is the "integration" of you and the alternative is what many of us are facing: *dis*-integration.

> ***The goal is the "integration" of you and the alternative is what many of us are facing: dis-integration.***

It's important to hear and feel the shame of all involved, inside and outside our own beings, for the shame cycle to end. Hearing the shame cycle of others is perhaps another definition of what empathy and compassion may actually be. To that end, the art of listening is next on my list of things I am practicing in my own battle.

LISTEN

Stephen Covey is best known in business and self-help circles for helping people become more successful personally and professionally. He's not a psychologist, he's a business person who has learned that listening to someone is like giving them emotional oxygen. This, as I argued before, is primarily because it interrupts the shame cycle of another person, which is horribly rare in our world.

In fact, it's so rare that you actually know exactly when it's happening. You know exactly when someone is actually listening to you because of how it feels. And, usually when it's over, you might just reflect on what an amazing person it is to have the ability to listen in that way. When we are listening, we are being compassionate. *Listening is perhaps the single most compassionate activity one can offer another human being.*

Listening also requires us to battle with our own shame, as well. When we are listening to listen and not to reply, we are acknowledging the possibility that the person we are listening to may be right. We are being vulnerable to the possibility we may not know everything about everything. We are open to growing and learning. To be open to the idea of growing and learning we are coming to grips, in a positive way, with the fact that we are imperfect.

When we are listening, we are also not talking. We are acknowledging that someone else matters in this moment. If your shame defense of choice is narcissism related, this will cause your shame defenses to rise as well and insist that you get your own air time in the conversation. This is your opportunity to acknowledge your own shame and then make your own decision to be compassionate and keep listening anyway.

> *...listening to someone is like giving them emotional oxygen.*

Moving forward is our goal—our fallibility is our perceived enemy—one we all share. When we are listening, we are not being defensive and we are in relationship. Being defensive is actually an act of self-sabotage because it prevents us from learning and growing and becoming as great as we actually are and, as long as we are truly listening, our defenses are at least on pause. A desire to grow, to move forward, to become what we hope, means acknowledging without hesitation and in courage that we are not enough and that it's actually OK, but we can only arrive there with defenses set aside.

By embracing defenselessness, by putting yourself in a position of vulnerability, you are daring the virus to show its head—you are taking the battle to the enemy to let it know that it has nowhere to hide. As soon as you open yourself to attack for your shortcomings or weaknesses, shame will have no choice but to come to your defense in whatever way it wants. That's when you own the conversation. You are now in charge of when shame arrives and it now serves you. But to make that happen will require us to listen.

Professing not to care what other people think about us or professing not to care about our own growth is not embracing defenselessness either, by the way. It's simply another symptom of the same virus. Whenever I would hear my girls say, "I don't even care what they think," I knew it was shame because they were ashamed at how weak they were to actually care. It *does* matter to us what people think and, if we set aside our defenses long enough to hear what they think, we might actually grow and improve and use it to empower our way to live in reality instead of the place where we are. One form of listening, to myself as well as others, is to read.

READ

At one point when I was getting my doctoral degree, the librarian at the seminary introduced our group of students to a new way of looking at books. When this librarian welcomed us into his world, he welcomed us to a slew of human beings waiting to have a conversation. These people, these authors, were all there to join us in the journey, not to teach us something but to join us. Each book he referred to as a "conversation partner."

If we understand that opening ourselves up to vulnerability involves being in relationships with people and attempting to retake what shame has stolen, we can see literature as one opportunity to become vulnerable, perhaps an easy first step along that path.

The opening paragraph from John Bradshaw's book is a great example. In his introduction to the book, Bradshaw admits his own battle with shame and immediately, I have a companion on the journey. I am writing a book very similar in theme to Bradshaw's but it's still another voice, another person, with whom you can converse. It's another voice that can tell you that you are not alone.

I sat with my son, Troy, one Saturday as he told me his story and it relieved me to know I was not alone in my own struggle. The next Monday I sat with another friend who recounted almost the exact same story as my son, with his own nuances and circumstances, and I was no less enthralled and encouraged. Books are the same way.

The fact that Bradshaw's book is out there, along with great pieces by any number of people, initially made me consider *not* writing what you are now reading. Really, 95% of the information I'm professing, authors already have addressed in their own way. There is literally nothing new under the sun when it comes to shame—it goes all the way back to Genesis!

However, if I did *not* write, we would not have met and would not be having the conversation we are now having. As I mentioned at the very beginning, a primary reason I'm writing this book is so that I can offer myself as a partner on your journey. Perhaps Bradshaw should also be your partner, or Brené Brown, or Robert Moore, or . . . the more the merrier!

I suppose I am just as hopeful that perhaps you will join me on my journey. Being together is the only hope we have for starving this virus out and finally living a life we direct ourselves, a life for our own good and the good of all creation.

Oddly, as I've read, I've received encouragement, companionship, and even empathy from the authors who have spoken to me through their work. How I can get empathy from an inanimate object I have no idea, but I feel heard when I read.

> *How I can get empathy from an inanimate object I have no idea, but I feel heard when I read.*

The most powerful example I have of this is the biography of Mother Teresa and the way it depicted her life in darkness (many may say depression but I think that underplays the condition and the estrangement she felt from God, in particular). When I heard Mother Teresa speak of the darkness and the pain from the profound sense of loss she was experiencing, I didn't feel alone. I felt heard amidst the challenges of my own life although I've never met her and never will. Somehow, we now are traveling together.

I want to pause here for a side note that will give you an indication how to hear shame when it comes calling. As I wrote those words about Mother Teresa, a voice of shame in my head tells me not to dare compare myself with Mother Teresa in any way, shape, or form. That voice of shame wants to prevent me from looking stupid in front of you. That voice wants to remind me of the greatness and sacrifice of Mother Teresa and the smallness of my own sacrifices in life compared to hers. Oddly, I don't think those are things Mother Teresa herself would ever have said to me. In fact, based on her own story, she had a pretty good self-hatred brewing in her own soul. It's quite clear from her own story that she considered herself the least of these and, frequently, an insincere fraud as well. Shame will rise whenever we are interacting with another human being, even if it is through books. That's what we want to happen. **We want to unmask it so we can disarm it.**

If, inside a book, you can find a place to find empathy, we should be rushing to them. While there is a vast array of empathy in books, one of the greatest and most valuable forms of empathy I have ever practiced is giving someone the benefit of the doubt.

BENEFIT OF THE DOUBT

There is a certain speech I give at corporate events regarding how to grow top line sales through customer appreciation. It's a play on words. We all know what it means to appreciate a customer for what they've bought from you—that's the old type of valuing individuals—by what they do for you.

Salespeople tend to be highly competitive people, which is an indication of a very strong shame response. Salespeople (of whom I am one) find their value in the sale, in the success, and primarily in the win. That said, any salesperson will tell you how humiliating it can be to be in sales. They will tell you stories of groveling in front of angry and unreasonable customers who do nothing but look down on them for being in sales—as if you work in child pornography or something vile such as that.

Unless you are on your guard, many salespeople may begin to develop a resentfulness toward their customers. This is because the other thing salespeople (and people in general) want is to be appreciated, and salespeople rarely are. It is much more frequent that they are looked down upon.

And soon you have developed a rather adversarial relationship with your clients, and are able to be successful only with the ones that like and appreciate you and only when you win or they win (to gain their appreciation).

Instead, I suggest that our relationships with our customers would improve if we sincerely appreciated our customers, as in "walked a mile in their shoes" sort of appreciating. What if we could appreciate where they are coming from when they are angry, dismissive, or condescending to realize that this is how they are expressing their own battle with shame? What if we were to appreciate the fact that they needed to make someone look small to make themselves feel good about who they are? Would that turn the tide in difficult customer relationships from being antagonistic to understanding?

What would happen if we could offer to our customers, our friends, our families, the opportunity to appreciate the possibility that the way they are lashing out at us, blaming us, getting defensive, throwing us under the bus, calling us fat, stupid, or ugly, is because they too are in their own hard battle with the shame raging inside themselves? Would that change our need to retaliate and our ability to stay in relationships?

What could happen if we didn't hit our kids when they "deserve it" because we appreciate the fact that they may want us to hit them because they think they "deserve it"? We can only arrive at this place if we can come to appreciate how shame is manipulating our own lives and the lives of those around us.

*　*　*

I was recently in a serious conflict with a coworker I didn't invite to a meeting I was holding. I didn't invite her to the meeting for a variety of reasons, mostly out of respect for her schedule and the fact we really didn't need her at the meeting.

She was crushed by the lack of invite and refused to talk with me. She, of course, assumed the worst, that I didn't want her there. Shame welled up inside her, suggesting that she was "not enough" and thereby was excluded from my meeting. She was hurt and confused by the whole thing to such an extent that it damaged our ability to work together even after I had apologized and explained myself to her. I'm quite certain she lost sleep over it for quite some time as a result of the internal battle she was in with herself.

What might have happened if she had given me the benefit of the doubt that maybe it wasn't about her? What if she had given me the benefit of the doubt that maybe I was actually attempting to be respectful of her time given the vast demands she was already facing? This, of course, would always be her challenge, as her internal shame calendar requires that she scour the calendars of all of us to find out where she's not invited to discern if she still has value, if she's still a contributor.

In the worst-case scenario—that I intentionally did not invite her because I didn't like anything about her—would she have the internal fortitude to not find her sense of well-being in my opinion of her even if that's exactly why I didn't invite her?

What if we were able to appreciate the path that each one of us walks that we may know nothing about? What amount of kindness could we offer instead of the self and mutual contempt we feel when our feelings get hurt by that person? What kind of world would that be if we could not only avoid having our own shame insist we take on other people's issues but that we could even be empathetic for the issue with which they are struggling? If we are, in fact, able to disarm this hidden driver that may be telling us things that aren't true, we may actually create a better world one human interaction at a time.

STOP COMPLAINING

Complaining is taking advantage of someone willing to listen to you and frequently generates additional shame in all involved.

Have you ever told someone how rough you have it at work? Here are my most frequent responses to that complaint.

1. **You think you have it bad, let me tell you about my job . . .**
2. **You should be grateful you have a job, I don't have one . . .**
3. **Yeah, I had a situation like that once . . .**

Complaining is chiefly a narcissistic endeavor that typically ends with the complainer feeling worse. What we are doing when we complain is insisting, in typically a rather infantile way, that someone pay attention to us, and it normally backfires. This is also a form of grandiosity sourced in shame that is always destined to leave us wanting.

I found that complaining soon creates what I call the "competitive complaint" in the person to whom you are complaining. When I complained, I found I would start a complaint competition with whomever I was speaking. If I had a hard job, they had a harder job. If I wasn't feeling well, they were feeling worse. It's as if, in my complaint of my hardship, I was dismissing their hardship. At the same time, when they would bring up their own complaint without acknowledging mine, I too felt dismissed until one of the two of us (typically me, I always felt) would stop to actually acknowledge the hardship of the other.

> *Complaining is chiefly a narcissistic endeavor that typically ends with the complainer feeling worse.*

Evidently, we all believe there's a sympathy shortage, so when you start grabbing for the sympathy that rightly belongs to you, your conversation partner will likely begin to grab for some of that sympathy as well before it's all used up. Ironically, when we are complaining, we may be looking for sympathy and not empathy. There's a huge difference that I don't have time to get into in this book but has been dealt with extensively by others.

It all reminds me of the child bouncing up and down on the diving board shouting to their parents to "Watch me, watch me!" Which makes all the sense in the world . . . when you're 9. The problem is many of us simply never had that childhood need met, so we still insist on a regular basis that someone pay attention to us. But we're not 9. Still, when we are not watched, we feel hurt, resentment, abandonment, and pain. And, if we dare acknowledge we feel these things, we can add shame to the list.

This is where it needs to come to our attention. Here is where we need to stop and ask ourselves why it is we need to inform someone of our complaint in life—what are we really attempting to gain?

I decided to quit complaining. No, I decided I had to quit. My complaints were cries from my shame, screaming to the world to notice me. And, as we all know, that cry frequently backfires when the one to whom you are complaining not only doesn't notice you, but insists that you, in fact, need to notice them. Ending my complaining became a Zorro circle of action.

Once I made the decision to stop complaining, I became *aware* of *how much* I do it! It's kind of like once you put a real budget together, you realize how much money you spend a month on going out to eat! Holy crap, did I complain! No wonder we have no resilience for complaining any more.

My complaints came in a number of disguises but were always intended to bring attention to some plight I was enduring.

1. **Venting: this is just a mechanism allowing me to transfer my anxiety to someone else.**
2. **Prayer requests: a favorite because it feels so holy when you're asking someone to pray for your this or that when your real intent is to inform people of your horrible state of affairs.**

3. **Informing interested parties: in this method, you actually convince yourself that people want to know, so you're doing them a favor by informing them of your complaints.**
4. **Demanding justice: your complaint is bigger than you!! This method makes me not a shame-based person looking for attention but rather a champion of the masses who has just been screwed by Delta's refusal to wait for you when you didn't show up in time to get through security.**

Anyway, it's amazing to see how much you have to complain about in life when you commit yourself to ending the practice and the vast array our complaints can take.

I've made quite a bit of progress in this area, although it's taken the better part of a couple years and, if I don't stay on my toes and I'm sitting between two very large people on an overcrowded airplane, I will quickly regress. Hopefully, when I hear the voice welling up, insisting I get noticed for whatever hardship I am suffering, I'm much more skilled at pausing and reassuring myself that misery doesn't really love company.

Since I have been making progress, I've attempted to expand my Zorro circle in this regard. I now realize that when other people are complaining to me, they have the same need I have—to simply be noticed by a world that doesn't give a shit about them. So, I do what they ask and what they deserve: I notice them. Sometimes, it's hard because in noticing *them,* I have to hear the voice of my shame insisting for my share of recognition, but this voice is growing dimmer as I get more skilled at just being nice. Shame is being unmasked and disarmed when I do what I want and not what it wants.

STOP THE SHAME BLAME GAME

I have saved the most punitive for last—the most destructive thing we can stop doing. Blame is the single most divisive event that can occur between humans, as I've already elaborated at length. Ironically, blame has never been more in front of us as Americans.

As I write this, America has just concluded the most bizarre and historic presidential elections, of our day. Front and center in that conversation was Donald Trump's insistence that the election was rigged and that he would only accept the results if he won.

While this pre-leveling of blame for a loss that had not yet even occurred was certainly a rarity, the post-leveling of blame knew regular and routine bounds.

Once the results became clear, Hillary Clinton was quick to level her blame on FBI director Comey who released word 11 days before the election that the investigation into Clinton's email situation was being reopened. She was also delighted to discover that the CIA was reporting that the Russians had intervened to help her lose the race. Finally, she was able to blame the Electoral College that gave the victory to Trump even though she won the raw voting by 2.8 million.

> *This ability to blame others for our losses will prevent us from actually learning something about ourselves.*

This ability to blame those outside ourselves for our losses will prevent us from actually learning something about ourselves. The ability to blame these outside forces will prevent the Democratic Party from coming to terms with the fact that it did not have a pulse on a majority of rural Americans and how they feel disenfranchised. Arkansas, Clinton's home state, was one of the biggest Trump supporters.

Trump, on the other hand, will be unable to acknowledge the Russians had anything to do with the election because it may mean he's not *as big* a winner as he'd like to believe. Further, he has had to find a way to discount Clinton's 2.8 million vote total "win" over him, which he's dismissed as illegal voting of one type or another.

The rise of Trump is also based on a need in our society to find blame. We blame China, India, and Mexico for taking our jobs—no, we blame our government for sending the jobs there. We blame immigrants and Islam and, as my daughters have discovered, African Americans for all our troubles. We need to find blame to prevent taking responsibility and to hold back the compassion we should feel for some of these poverty-ridden nations because no one has felt compassion for us when we lost our jobs to them.

Ironically, blame was also the first thing out of Adam's mouth when God came looking for him in the garden. When asked who had told him he was naked, Adam—whose name itself is synonymous with all of humanity—blames "the woman you gave me." Ironically, Adam gets a two-fer here with this excuse.

1. **He can blame the woman but also**
2. **He can blame God for providing this deceitful creature to lead him astray.**

Shame dictates that we find another source for our "not enoughness," which has landed us in whatever hole we find ourselves.

We have mocked Donald Trump for his desire to shift blame from any appearance of loss, but it's a fairly common practice even if we aren't as bold as Mr. Trump. It's what we all do because we all carry shame and it's what shame insists of us.

When the ministry I was leading came to an end, it was certainly in my heart—a need I had—to blame someone or something. When something like that happens, you can blame the denomination for not giving you enough support, you can blame the congregation for not trying harder, you can blame the economy, the location, and, as always, you can blame God Almighty for calling you to something that was destined to fail. In the end, I tried them all and, frankly, finding blame gave me some relief, but it gave me no healing.

The historically popular tendency to find a human 'other' to serve as a scapegoat for explanation of the impact of evil in our lives, one who can serve as a receptacle for our shadow projections, and who, if they are imprisoned, tortured, burned, bombed, and so forth, can be used as ritual sacrificial victims to give us a bogus sense of mastery over our desperate situation (Moore 2003, 2).

You can also blame yourself.

Blaming yourself is different than the healthy version of coming to grips with the reality of being a human being with limitations. Self-blame is a form of self-contempt or self-hatred, which, instead of seeing your imperfections as a gift, making you aware of your humanity, is a curse making you aware of your "not enoughness."

Remember that shame is nearly synonymous with self-hatred, so when we attempt to shift blame elsewhere, it's so we are not discovered for the loser we, consciously or subconsciously, believe we are. Those of us who have some awareness of our self-hatred are quick and decisive in where blame ultimately lay, with us and our inadequacies.

This is likely the greatest challenge of anyone who has attempted to read thus far. Someone unaware of the degree to which they blame themselves and is still blaming others has likely stopped reading. Herein, however, lies the greatest challenge.

Every day, with each event of life, we will have an opportunity to assign blame. Resisting the tendency and, instead, asking ourselves why we really need to assign blame—to ourselves or someone else— in a given situation may actually shine light on the shame attempting to manipulate us. Shame with light on it must release you from its grip, and your refusal to do what it wants means it is being disarmed and you are running your own life.

CONCLUSION

The Road to Redemption and Reconciliation

Lastly, I just want to leave you with something I've learned in this process, as well. I feel like we all have two battles, with two enemies going on: one with the man across from you; the second is with the man inside of you. I think once you control the one inside of you, the one across from you really doesn't matter. And I think that's what we're all trying to do. —Tony Romo, on probably losing his starting QB job (MSNBC 2016)

I have attempted to address some key points on shame using my own story:

1. **Shame is the primary motivator behind our poor decisions.**
2. **Shame has affected every human in recorded history.**

189

3. The symptoms or defenses we construct vary in type and degree.
   • These defenses are what create the destruction
4. There are some key points to managing the situation:
   • Acknowledge the enemy within and understand how it operates.
   • Enter the battle through shame awareness that only comes through community and testing your own shame responses inside that community.
5. The outcome of being shame resilient will be an ever-increasing ability to make the decisions you want to make for yourself and becoming a more empathetic and compassionate person. In short, living the life you want to live.

I believe the primary motivating force behind our self-destructive decisions and choices flows from a fountain I call shame, the voice of which is trying in one way or another to remind you that you are not enough *and force you to do something about it.*

It's in our constant battle to become enough—a condition at which we will never arrive because we are human—that we may make choices we will forever regret. Those choices can range from the mundane such as picking your career to the catastrophic such as taking your own life or abusing your child. But, as the woman in the Garden of Eden showed us, grasping for the apple of enoughness is the story of all humanity.

> *It's in our constant battle to become enough—a condition at which we will never arrive because we are human—that we may make choices we will forever regret.*

While we are all hunting for enoughness, what we most likely truly *want* is redemption, and what we *need* is reconciliation.

REDEMPTION

We want to know that something will come of our story, that even our failings and our "not enoughness" will ultimately be helpful for ourselves and our children. I think what we all want to believe is that this will end well regardless of how it looks in this moment.

Ironically, we all know this for other people. We all have seen repeatedly how failure and shortcomings and a willingness to be vulnerable have consistently led to redemption—to something great coming out of weakness. Frequently, we admire those who have dared to be vulnerable and dared to fail, wishing we had such courage. For those of us who are Christian, it is the very heart of our entire religious system. Still, we frequently find it hard to believe for ourselves.

Redemption sounds like a one-time event from which there is never a stumbling once it happens, you are either free or enslaved. Perhaps that happens to some, but most of us, I think, fall into another camp. Most of us live in a camp where our constant flow of mistakes, failures, and weaknesses lead us on a path of continued growth and maturing into what it means to be a human being if we are able to disarm the voice of shame that is attempting to prevent it from happening.

The evidence I've seen in my own experiences suggests we don't arrive at redemption any more than we arrive at intelligence or maturity—it's something we grow into and become. I still believe, in that model, there's plenty of space in which God may be our redeemer, but it's not via a magic wand, as much as it is from walking our own path or, as it's been said, carrying our own cross *daily*.

RECONCILIATION

Our goal is to "disarm" this hidden driver behind our destructive decisions, not to annihilate it. While I have used some fairly negative words to describe this hidden driver (shame) such as "the enemy within," venom, a virus, etc., we must also recognize it is

> *Our goal is to "disarm" this hidden driver behind our destructive decisions, not to annihilate it.*

part of us and it can create an inner war to realize the "enemy" is part of us.

I see in myself and my fellow shame travelers what appears to be a constant inner conflict within ourselves against this invader that is literally part of us. The problem, as I mentioned, is that it is not an invader, and to war with yourself can end up in very bad places as well. Our goal in *disarming* this driver is to prevent it from doing damage to ourselves or others.

As a result of disarming this driver, we may be able to call a truce within ourselves and end the war. We may be able to *integrate* all the parts of our lives and even the history that has perhaps brought us so much pain instead of *dis-integrating*. This is critical because truly healthy living can only take place in an integrated person. Dis-integrating leads exactly where it sounds like it leads. There is much written on this topic but is beyond the scope of what we can accomplish in this particular work. It will be saved for another day.

ONE DAY AT A TIME

I had lunch with my youngest daughter, Tapricia, just before Christmas this last year, and she was describing this war within herself and asked me if I knew anyone who had overcome shame. She asked me if I knew anyone who had become like Jesus in his ability to not seem to care what other people thought of him—to be at final peace with who you are. She asked if I really ever knew anyone who had been able to be vulnerable in that way—to be fully content with their humanness and not have an inner need to defend themselves or tear other people down.

I had to confess that I have not. But, I also said I wasn't sure that was the goal. I went back to my argument about Zorro circles and said that I think the best any of us can hope for is to win the battle of this moment. To be able to not project our false self or pretense of something we want others to think we are *in this moment*. I said it might simply be enough to hear and contradict that voice of shame *in this moment* to make the decisions we want to make *in this moment*.

This model describes a moment-by-moment process of disarming shame—perhaps easier for some and harder for others—but a process nonetheless. It seems to me much more of a narrow road than a wide road, a road less traveled. It definitely seems like a road that is nearly impossible to travel alone.

On this road, however, it's not just a resilience to shame we hope to achieve but the evolution of something about us from what may have once appeared as scornful and bad to something redeemed and reconciled to be strong, beautiful, and hopeful.

I have little doubt that this story, my story, may be dismissed or even mocked by some as *navel gazing*—a term intended to refer to unfruitful introspective activity. When these accusations are leveled against me, I will feel the need to defend myself—I actually already do! I will feel the need to convince them that I am right and they are wrong. That is how I will feel. So, this too will remind me that the accuser is not, in fact, the person sitting across from me but is the person within.

But, for right now and today, I will tell my story in hopes that it resonates with you and that, perhaps, you will join me in the battle to embrace our humanity, our insufficiency, our "not enoughness," so that, together, we are not alone. Having called out this hidden driver, perhaps, together, we can begin to celebrate being us and the gifts of our imperfections so that we can begin living our own lives instead of the lives the world insists we live. Perhaps we can begin making the decisions and choices in this moment, and then the next, and then the next . . . that will lead to health not only for us but our families, our friends, our enemies, and people all over this very small and very similar race we call humanity.

I hope this has been a suitable traveling partner for you on your road to redemption and reconciliation. It has certainly not been the first such offering on this subject, and I'm sure won't be the last, as we will all need frequent reminders from a variety of voices along the way. I'm glad to have traveled with you thus far.

2 Corinthians 12 [8] Three times, I pleaded with the Lord to take it [my weakness] away from me. [9] But he said to me, "My grace is sufficient for you, for my power is made perfect in weakness." Therefore, I will boast all the more gladly about my weaknesses, so that Christ's power may rest on me. [10] That is why, for Christ's sake, I delight in weaknesses, in insults, in hardships, in persecutions, in difficulties. For when I am weak, then I am strong. — The Apostle Paul

Bibliography

Achor, Shawn. *The Happiness Advantage: The Seven Principles that Fuel Success and Performance at Work.* New York: Virgin Books; 2011.

Agassi, Andre. *Open: An Autobiography.* New York: Vintage; 2009.

Bloomberg TV. *Bloomberg Game Changers: Steve Jobs.* Bloomberg TV; 2010. Available at: https://www.bloomberg.com/news/videos/b/0669fda9-a487-42ab-8e68-3025d1ed4a1a. Accessed February 28, 2017.

Bradshaw, John. *Healing the Shame that Binds You.* Deerfield Beach, FL: Health Communications, Inc; 2005.

Brown, Brené. *I Thought It Was Just Me (But it Isn't): Making the Journey from "What Will People Think?" to "I Am Enough."* New York: Penguin; 2008.

Brown, Brené. *The Gifts of Imperfection: Let Go of Who You Think You're Supposed to Be and Embrace Who You Are.* Center City, MN: Hazelden Publishing; 2010.

Capps, Donald. *The Depleted Self: Sin in a Narcissistic Age.* Minneapolis, MN: Fortress Press; 1993.

cummings, e. e. "Advice to a student poet." Ottawa Hills High School *Spectator.* Grand Rapids, MI: October 26, 1955.

Gilbert, Elizabeth. Big Magic: Creative Living Beyond Fear. New York: Riverhead Books; 2016.

Hybels, Lynne, and Bill Hybels. *Rediscovering Church.* Grand Rapids, MI: Zondervan; 1995.

Jung, Carl. *Modern Man in Search of a Soul.* San Diego, CA: Harcourt Harvest; 1955.

Kaufman, Gershen. *Shame: The Power of Caring,* 3rd edition, rev. and expanded. Rochester: Schenkman Books, Inc.; 1992.

Lasch, Christopher. *The Culture of Narcissism: American Life in an Age of Diminishing Expectations.* New York: W. W. Norton & Company, Inc.; 1991.

McNish, Jill L. *Transforming Shame: A Pastoral Response.* Binghampton: The Haworth Pastoral Press; 2004.

Moore, Robert L. *Facing the Dragon Confronting Personal and Spiritual Grandiosity.* Wilmett, IL: Chiron Publications; 2003.

MSNBC. *Tony Romo's deep, emotional message might make you cry.* November 15, 2016. Available at: http://www.msn.com/en-us/sports/nfl/tony-romos-deep-emotional-message-might-make-you-cry/ar-AAklAs9?li=BBnb7Kz. Accessed February 28, 2017.

Palmer, Parker. *The Courage to Teach.* San Francisco: Jossey-Bass Inc.; 1997.

O'Neill, Hugh. "How to Have a Midlife Crisis." July 11, 2003. *Men's Health.* Available at: http://www.menshealth.com/health/midlife-crisis.

Peck, M. Scott. *The Road Less Traveled: A New Psychology of Love, Traditional Values and Spiritual Growth.* New York: Simon and Schuster; 1978.

Peterson, Eugene H. *Under the Unpredictable Plant An Exploration in Vocational Holiness.* Grand Rapids, MI: Eerdman's; 1992.

Reingold, Jennifer. "Hondas in Space." February 1, 2005. Available at: https://www.fastcompany.com/52065/hondas-space. Accessed March 12, 2017.

Rogers, Justin. "Matt Millen reflects on not sticking to his guns as Detroit Lions CEO in NFL Network documentary."

October 8, 2013. Available at: http://www.mlive.com/lions/index.ssf/2013/10/matt_millen_a_football_life.html. Accessed March 12, 2017.

Rohr, Richard. *Falling Upward: A Spirituality for the Two Halves of Life*. San Francisco: Josey Bass; 2011.

Rollins, Henry. "Henry Rollins: Football, Violence, and America." February 14, 2013. *LA Weekly*. Available at: http://www.laweekly.com/content/printView/4170187.

Shannon, William H., ed. *Hidden Ground of Love: The Letters of Thomas Merton on Religious Experience and Social Concerns*. San Diego, CA: Harcourt; 1993.

Thompson, Curt. *The Soul of Shame*. Downers Grove, IL: Intervarsity Press; 2015.

Warren, Rick. *The Purpose Driven Church*. Grand Rapids: Zondervan; 1995.

About the Author

The breadth of Rick Patterson's life experiences and education have contributed greatly to this book. Rick earned a bachelor's degree in engineering and spent his early career years in sales, sales team management, and business development for an international chemical company. He returned to school to receive his master's of divinity degree and became an ordained minister.

He and his wife adopted a sibling group of four children, which facilitated his departure from corporate America and into ministry full time. Rick spent the next 10 years in new church development for his denomination and earned his doctoral degree in ministry. In 2011, Rick returned to corporate America where he's employed as a platform launch manager in the paper industry.

While he wrote his doctoral dissertation on how shame motivates and manipulates our lives, it is the compilation of these life experiences and his own battles with the enemy within that opened his eyes to the pervasive impact of shame across religious, professional, racial, gender, and generational lines. The author of *Shame Unmasked,* Rick frequently speaks and writes about how people can disarm shame to regain control of their lives.

88831319R00122

Made in the USA
Columbia, SC
12 February 2018